STEALING
Life in America

STEALING
Life in America

A Collection of Essays By

MICHELLE CACHO-NEGRETE

Adelaide Books
New York/ Lisbon

2017

STEALING: Life in America
A Collection of Essays
By Michelle Cacho-Negrete

Copyright © 2017 By Michelle Cacho-Negrete

Published by Adelaide Books, New York / Lisbon
An imprint of the Istina Group DBA
adelaidebooks.org

Editor-in-Chief
Stevan V. Nikolic

For any information, please address Adelaide Books
at info@adelaidebooks.org

ISBN13: 978-0-9995164-1-6
ISBN10: 0-9995164-1-8

Printed in the United States of America

For
my mother Jean Goodman
who taught me to believe in possibilities
and my husband Kevin Smith
who helped me make possibilities a reality

Acknowledgements

I am grateful to Michael Steinberg, the best mentor/teacher a writer could have. Thanks to Ragdale where some of these essays were written. Gratitude to my exacting readers, Susan O'Neil, Kelley Brennan, Krista Bremer, Jenny Doughty, Alice Lowe, Gina Troisi, Lesley Heiser, Jodi Paloni, Virginia Mackey, Terri Sutton, all themselves wonderful writers. Thanks to the magazines that published me, in particular Sy Safransky and the Sun Staff, and Lee Hope of Solstice Literary Magazine. A very special thanks to Stevan and Adelaide Nikolic for publishing and promoting this book. Lastly I'd like to thank my family for their endless support: Carl and Deide, Bruce and Lise, and the very best grandchildren, Micaela, Cole, Sadie, Ceiligh. A very special acknowledgement to Don, Terry and Mike who have kept me going for 30 frigid Maine winters. Lastly, to my beloved brother Bruce Ted, who would have had stories of his own.

Michelle Cacho-Negrete

Contents

Stealing

The day I decided to steal food I instituted three simple rules: Steal only essentials, only from big chains, never brag. Although I'd not stolen for twenty years or so, it was immediately familiar, reviving an edgy competence that kept me street-smart in suburbia, seventy miles from the Brooklyn ghetto I'd grown up in. I'd stolen food from the age of eight until roughly the age of fourteen, the $50.00 my mother earned weekly incapable of providing what we needed. My first theft, conducted with breathless impulsivity, was at the corner grocery. On the way to school one morning, my brother and I paused to stare lustfully at bins of bagels piled high in a large glass window. The yeasty inviting smell leaked out the door as customers went in and out.

Warning my brother to wait outside, I slipped inside the store, the bell that announced me lost in the laughter of the owner and a neighborhood woman, and left, unnoticed, with four bagels in my pocket. The bagels were freshly baked, their residual warmth against my body a promise of pleasure to come. We devoured them on the way to school, poking moist fingertips into my pocket to capture every crumb.

My success at filling our growling stomachs that morning led me to begin raiding the near-by chain supermarket, stuffing shiny tins of fish, small rolls and crisp vegetables into my pocket. That winter I passed a store window with a pair of warm leather boots nestled in drifts of ersatz fur and jewels. I visited the store next day in my oldest pair of loafers and left wearing the boots. That winter I would steal a blue woolen dress, a heavy coat, two albums by the Weavers, two shirts, boots and warm jacket for my brother before acquiring a summer job at fourteen. The job led to a part time one after school that provided enough money for what I needed, putting an end to my career as thief.

My adult poverty, living in the middle-class, painfully stereotypic Long Island suburb my ex-husband had moved our two sons and ourselves to before our divorce, seemed bleak enough to me after we separated to resurrect the practice; it was easier than I'd imagined. I never fit into this enclave he'd chosen of matching sheets and dishes, ritualized family dinners at seven o'clock, coffee klatches to discuss delicate marital details, an insistence that a certain social acceptance depended upon the ownership of redundant items or useless absurdities. My neighbors favored manicured nails, artfully disheveled hair lacquered with hairspray, over-priced clothing designed to suggest a wanton bohemian freedom: jeans artfully ripped at the knees and fine cotton shirts streaked with paint. I found it deceitful in the particularly American way that later encouraged affluent teenagers to affect the street style of the ghetto as though mere appearance altered the life they'd been born into, a sly way to present the credentials of the scarred without the pain and inconvenience. I still drank tea from glasses as my immigrant mother had, dressed in comfortable, unfashionable clothes, carried a backpack, my lack of concern with appearances provoking both distance and an odd envy from a few of my neighbors. I felt myself differentiated from those around me through a form of natural selection that insured survival, a reverse snobbery as an antidote to not belonging. My ex-husband, with his history of coolly tiled rooms and attentive servants before fleeing Cuba, liked to say, "You can take the girl out of the slum, but not the slum out of the girl." His desire for a return to upper-middle-class existence was finally realized with a more acceptable wife, in another small house in another small suburb identical to this one. We were both thieves since, while married, we had stolen each other's sense of certainty, a theft finally remedied by our divorce.

My ex-husband, vengeful about the divorce, reluctantly paid rent and minimum child support. He could not be cajoled or pleaded with when I ran short of money at the end of the month; he was immune to guilt. I was in college full-time by then, certain an education could insure freedom from poverty. My income, besides what he contributed, came from a work-study job teaching problem kids, a pittance from baking for college bakeries, student loans, a scholarship; a lot of work that barely provided enough to buy gas and pay bills. The only government service available to us was the free lunch program for my sons. I had no access to the far more acceptable white-collar crime, the art of acquiring luxury through manipulation. The choice was easy. Hunger defined my childhood; it would not define that of my children's nor my old age. I would not quit school for a low-paying job, and we would not be hungry.

One Saturday, while my sons visited their father, I cased the nearby supermarket. I shopped there, purchasing bruised produce, day-old breads, items marked down a day before their expiration date. Childhood hunger fostered the concept of food as a precious commodity. I shopped for peaches, apples, pears, peppers, broccoli, asparagus, the way other women might shop for expensive jewelry, the green of a smooth, full pepper as exotic as an emerald.

The scent of the store was intoxicating, prompting regression to a ten-year-old child who was starving despite having eaten lunch one-half-hour earlier. I breathed deeply as though smell could sate my hunger then stuffed free samples into my mouth regardless of what they were. After that, I sank into sheer instinct, a shark targeting nutrition-rich items like tuna that would easily fit in my pockets, under-sized vegetables that would lie flat against my body, a can of dough that baked up into warm, tasteless rolls. I avoided frozen foods, which would leave widening stains of moisture as the frost melted. Containers of milk were the most difficult but the taste of powdered milk was onerous; it was the taste of poverty. On my way out I slid a container into my pocket, hooking my arm in a particular way to conceal it.

I exited the store prideful as anyone completing a job successfully, pleased that my skills, dormant for so many years, were intact, like riding a bike. I left the store warning myself not to feel too confident, to remain cautious. Each succeeding theft would increase my chance of being caught – the law of averages, something I was taught by my step-father, a professional gambler long-vanished from my life.

Often, before driving home from my work-study job at a private school in an up-scale neighborhood, I would peruse their supermarkets, noting the better cuts of meat, fresher vegetables, exotic fruit, pocketing items not easily available. This supermarket was easier to pilfer than the one in my neighborhood, as if hands-on stealing was inconceivable in a community of gracious houses with gardeners and cleaning women.

That winter I stole each son a winter coat, putting them, one at a time, over my thin jacket and leaving the department store without incident. I also entered with an empty shopping bag and left with two sets of boots, prices ripped off; smeared with dirt to suggest I'd just retrieved them from the store's shoe repair shop.

I stole food for approximately two years, branching out to include frozen vegetables by stuffing a plastic bag in each of my pockets. I found a job the week before I graduated with a BS in education. I stole my last day's worth of meals before my first paycheck. When I was paid, we went out to a restaurant for dinner. We each had three deserts.

I moved to Maine two months after graduation, needing distance from my ex-husband's hostility. I accepted a low-paying job at a rural school for disabled children simply because they were first to contact me. I'd never before had directions given in terms of trees, family farmhouses, clocks with cracked faces on old church steeples. The students' parents worked outside jobs, hunted for deer or moose to provide meat, put up fruits and vegetables from their gardens. Often, I was gifted with cuts of venison, which although a vegetarian myself I would cook up for my sons. These parents possessed an innate generosity, a quality I'd often experienced back in Brooklyn, an axiom proven true, that those with little were often likely to help each other.

The school, with little state funding, went broke a month before the end of the school year. New teachers were rarely hired in mainstream schools before the end of August. My ex-husband, who had remarried, was clear that there'd be no loan to tide me over. I was alone, felt robbed of those closest to me through a systemic lack of services and conscience: my mother had died in a charity ward, lacking proper medical care after a flawed surgery. My brother had been killed in Vietnam, unable to flee to Canada nor escape service through attending college as those of means did. I was frightened by this replication of my mother's situation; two children to feed and no husband, felt trapped in the cycle of poverty I'd witnessed in the ghetto, the possibility of escape dangling just out of reach.

I quickly found a job as a saleswoman in an overpriced craft store in a plush resort town, bursting with tourists who skied in winter and swam in their second-home pools in summer. Each morning on the way to work I passed chic people carrying bags filled with newly purchased, non-essential items. I beat back my ghetto child's resentment, reminding myself that my goal was to achieve a status that allowed me the choice of not purchasing such things. My salary was meager; the job designed for college students from the town whose parents had connections, their employment an easy introduction to the working world, their salary merely "pin money." Affluent America displayed itself around me each morning, a glittery landscape without scorched edges. The nation felt broken in some irretrievable way, the founding ideals, the myth of opportunity and equality, the promise that a college education granted food on the table, seemed a deliberate distraction from the nation's essential truth; certain elements of the population would always be deprived, reaffirmed thirty years later with the wreckage of Katrina. I viewed the lies the government told us about Vietnam, and Watergate as smaller lies, both transient and inevitable, swapping out one scandal or war for the next that would surely come. They seemed to me a greater conspiracy of lies; the false promises that kept the working class, continually hopeful of a break-through into wealth that rarely happened. I saw the government engaged in a delicate balancing act to mythologize possibility despite the rarity of actualization.

I hated my bitterness, my cynicism, my recurrent anger, but especially hated hunger, its continuing saga almost blinding me to a specific reality, that the fruits of my education were only temporarily on vacation and quietly waiting for the end of summer to get back to work. While I would never be wealthy, I would be able to pay bills. The country was not in a recession, a depression or any other financial crisis; I was simply out of a job. I needed to make it through four months after which I would likely be hired to teach.

I had too much to lose to risk stealing again – no school would hire a teacher with a criminal record. I thought about a second job. It was the casual conversation between a pair of customers as I wrapped their purchases that provided an answer: The Happy Hour. The description of the bounty they'd consumed for the price of cocktails was compelling. I'd never gone to bars, had no actual knowledge beyond advertisements I'd ignored, of this teasing come-on, this offering of succulent shrimp, spare ribs, fried rice; salty food designed to encourage the consumption of liquor.

Philosophically, is ordering three cokes so you can fill your paper plate four or five times stealing food? Is it in the amorphous gray area that informs so many interpretations? We ate far more than the cost of our cokes, yet the liquor others consumed was so expensive that our meals were already paid for. My stepfather would have said that "the house" has all the advantages, so do your best to win.

Our first visit was a revelation. We went to a bar attached to a well-reviewed Chinese restaurant. The heavy metal door opened onto a stratum of sounds piled atop each other like players at a football skirmish: loud conversations, waitresses' shouting orders, a basketball game on television, all balanced on a foundation of jazz. The smell of food was tainted by cigarette smoke and all around us was that certain boozy indulgence of drinking freely manifested by lopsided smiles and loud laughs.

We passed the hot-table and gasped at the bounty: carrots, broccoli, cauliflower, cheese, spare ribs, fried chicken wings, grapes, watermelon, cantaloupe and strawberries out of season, tiny slices of chocolate cake. I was giddy with the offering, my perpetually starving child nearly wild with excitement. To this day, that table remains vivid in my memory, exaggerated through time into a cornucopia of food overflowing the bins, the rising perfume of grease, garlic and soy sauce, a sacrament for the deserving. We found a table and I designed a balanced menu for us. The waitress brought our cokes while we heaped our plates as high as possible. She returned after our third refill at the hot table and with a wink refilled our cokes as well.

On the way home, in the warmth of my old Honda, we joked about being so full we had stomachaches, even critiquing the food we'd filled our plates with again and again, pointing out what was overdone, what was too salty, how dried-out the cheese was, fruit not quite ripe. I felt drunk, experienced an unexpected power, had a fraudulent belief that I'd "gamed the system," as my stepfather would describe it; the slum child's desire to win on her own terms.

We developed an itinerary. Mondays the Chinese restaurant, Tuesdays and Thursdays a bar my sons labeled "The designer cream cheese place," with five cream cheese spreads, fresh vegetables, crackers and fruit, Wednesdays an Italian restaurant offering tiny meatballs, fried eggplant, and sautéed green and red peppers. Friday and Saturday were big happy hour nights, an overflow of rich salty food obscene in their plentitude. I wanted my mother then, dead two years, to experience this over-indulgence. I wanted to lift her from the debris of gaunt survival through the petty expense of overpriced coke. I mourned that she knew nothing of this possibility back then, however the shabby neighborhood bars of my childhood most likely offered nothing more than scratchy jukebox recordings and chipped glass ashtrays. My mother, an immigrant woman with a sixth grade education, fluent in five languages, self-taught and well read, would never have ventured into an upscale bar. She labored as a file clerk for the American Kennel Club, an organization devoted to owners of show dogs that cost more than one year of her salary. Sunday offered no happy hours, but we got by on what I'd stuffed into my purse at the previous days.

That summer, so long ago, was the last one of need. I slowly acquired the trappings of comfort; a second husband, a house, vacations, and a full refrigerator. My consciousness remains working class: clothing from second hand stores, staples rather than prepared food, cynical view of the culture. I have, however, acquired excess: ten cashmere sweaters at three dollars each but still eight more than I need, two dozen crystal wineglasses from Good Will, though I have barely a dozen friends, two winter coats though one is enough.

Fifteen years ago an overweight woman in my writing group discussed her diet, taking personal responsibility for overeating since nobody starves in America. Everyone else nodded. I was shocked, as though plunged into ice water, to realize I had achieved a level of affluence that allowed me to join a group that espoused this distortion. I felt displaced, free-floating, seduced by the diamond-bright glint of sun on the ocean, the sunlight through the green canopy of trees, the vanquishing of personal hunger. I'd slipped into a world of truth different than my own; that hunger is an everyday affair and stealing can be another way to make a living.

An unexpected surge of anger knotted my throat, anger I hadn't felt in years. I envied these women their parents and siblings, their paid college education after high school, their freedom to have refused jobs they didn't want, but especially their certainty that the system worked on their behalf. I reminded myself their class was an accident of birth not a choice, what my stepfather would have called a roll of the dice. I realized then how stranded I was in the midst of a failed metamorphosis; my consciousness one of sordid memories where rats chewed holes in the walls of apartments, my circumstance one of middle-class comforts. I felt myself a traitor, my anger primarily at myself rather than those who casually accepted their lifestyle as their right.

In that group the following week I wrote an essay about growing up hungry, about stealing food. Silence ensued as I used words usually confined to the perimeter of polite conversation: class, hunger, poverty. I understood in their silence that I had stolen the most precious thing that could be taken from these intelligent women; their flimsy pretext that nobody is hungry in America. I was tarnished; my differences previously labeled eccentric, quaint, Bohemian, now recognized as deviant. While they'd known that I had grown up in a ghetto, they'd never contemplated what that actually meant; the poor either villainized or romanticized in film; propaganda to assuage the conscience of "the other America." They felt attacked by this explosion of detail, the burst of anger on the page, my house, my smooth-running car, my excess of cashmere sweaters, all revealed as concealment of a vital fact; I was not one of them. They never voiced their anger with me, but it was evident in the way they turned away and within a few months I left group. Eventually I moved, met other women, developed friendships, learned to be easier with possessions, although I sometimes wander my house, touch things, wonder what I am doing owning all of this.

But I do own all of this; I am the fruition of the American dream. I am an American fairytale come true. I am the bastard child of poverty and perfect timing, a product of one of those periodic windows of opportunity, in this instance Lyndon Johnson's vision of the Great Society that offered scholarships, free lunch for children, a college counselor to guide me through an alien world. It is my grandchildren who are the ultimate culmination of the American dream, offspring of a peculiar type of immigrant, one who has never left their native country, merely emigrated from one class to another. They are a first generation who has never known poverty and can comfortably speak the language of their native landscape; their parents safely crossed the border but they are the true citizens. I remain an immigrant, poverty my country of origin. I cannot comfortably navigate this new land of enough, often speaking out of turn, committing cultural faux-pas', seeped in survivor guilt, I am a *class* act, a victim, perhaps volitional, of the final theft of belonging somewhere.

Street Kid

We were not *children*: we were *kids*, street kids, keys around our necks, sole-worn shoes, clothes too big or too small. Our landscape was gray, a defeated composition of concrete, asphalt and faded blacktop coated with the oil of a thousand leaking cars. The air was nearly unbreathable, permanently soiled from the smokestacks lining the neighborhood and spewing poison. We lived in tenements that leaned against each other for protection, their plastic-covered windows blind eyes in winter that popped open in spring to spy into each other's apartments. The hallways stunk from piss, pot, cheap perfume, cigarettes. Our lives were a confluence of shit jobs, vanished fathers, gang violence, junkies nodding off in hallways, a matrix of *stranded.*

Just across the bridge was the exalted landscape of Manhattan, an elegant spread of penthouses and doormen, gourmet food shops, discreet jewelry stores, expensive restaurants and one of the world's best art museums. We didn't belong there and it didn't matter; we were defiantly proud of not belonging and claimed the status of outsider with arrogance.

We were expected to accomplish nothing more than to replace our parents, to remain as stagnant as the air. Evolution was not for us. The schools reinforced that lesson: girls must be waitresses, saleswomen, file clerks, underage mothers, the boys construction workers, truckers, dock workers, or drunks rolling out of the bars at one in the morning. We were expected to occupy those same tenements, have those same low paying jobs, birth children we couldn't afford, die of lung cancer, liver ailments, childbirth, or from the ubiquitous diseases of violence: stabbings, beatings, drug overdoses, shootings. It was the fifties, before John Lindsay and Robert Kennedy, and no city politician considered us important enough to find a cure. Although we glimpsed a middle-class world on television, in movies, in magazines, we'd been assigned our societal roles: to be manifestations of a bogeyman's threat to those who didn't listen to their parents, or the police, or anybody in power. We were examples of what failure looked like. Our poverty was un-American, a stain against the country's good name. Middle-class children lived in houses with yards on Long Island, or apartments with sunny windows, but the tenements were our home.

Except they weren't; the streets were. The streets confirmed that we were in an unnamed war (until Johnson named it *the war on poverty*). They trained us in survival, in how to avoid being beaten or raped and master stealing food, clothing, shoes, records, radios. We didn't understand until years later that our thievery played into the hands of those who proclaimed us beyond redemption, that tax money was better spent elsewhere.

We periodically attended school, although what was the use? Any academic knowledge seemed taught us by mistake; our futures had been planned three generations ago. Only our mothers disputed those futures. They left and came home in the dark stooped from low-waged jobs, long subway rides, too much time on their feet. They cooked eggs or spaghetti or fatty hamburgers garnished with not quite spoiled vegetables and bread with moldy edges sliced off. They asked us about school while they washed dishes and assessed with defeated eyes what was left in the refrigerator until payday. They were proud of us, imagining we still attended school, that we would attend college, have lives different than their own, while the school guidance counselors said we'd be lucky to get a high school diploma.

Our mothers were certain we would succeed, even the schizophrenic mother who heard secret messages from the radio, even the one on welfare, even the two leveled out by alcohol, even the two mothers, including mine, who tried stretch their salaries to cover a week's worth of meals. We knew we already had; we survived. We were scornful of those middle-class children who couldn't predict a gang rumble, or steal food, or know the safe streets. Yet for all our scorn we secretly imagined that if we were patient and paid attention and became really good mimics, we might one day pass for them; we might one day succeed in their world. We secretly imagined our mothers might be right.

There were six of us who didn't remember a time when we hadn't known each other's faces, each other's voices, each other's mothers and the two fathers who occasionally visited, and the sisters and brothers both alive and dead. We had history. When we were little, the girls cuddled dolls with stringy hair and dirty faces while we sat on the tenement steps. We played house with cartons we found on the streets and yelled in our mother's voices *to just behave for God's sake.* The boys smashed each other with battered GI Joes uttering loud angry "fucks" when a leg or arm dropped off in ghostly premonition of Vietnam. They collided matchbox cars with missing wheels. They stood over each other threateningly and warned to *shut the fuck up and do what you are told or else* while they raised imaginary belts.

When we were older, we played skully in the gutters, relishing the snap of the bottle caps, their slide to the fading chalk boxes, raising our middle fingers to the drivers that hollered from car windows to *get the fuck out of the street.* We built scooters from old roller skate wheels and wood from construction sites, then careened past churches and grocery stores where men played dominos outside, past bars with the stink of booze floating out on a blue nicotine haze, narrowly avoided mothers pushing babies in second-hand strollers, circled boys who harmonized on songs by The Platters or The Drifters and hoped to be somehow, miraculously, discovered. One winter we built zip guns from rubber bands, splintered wood, and cut-up bits of linoleum we found behind a factory, shooting sharp pieces across the gutter at each other, ducking behind parked cars. We played handball in the court across the street from the big bank where our parents deposited three dollars every week into Christmas clubs, the money ultimately used for gas, electricity, a doctor bill, food.

We crowded together on the fire escapes that overlooked the street, read Peyton Place to each other, listened to Alan Freed on a staticky radio and yelled down to schoolmates that we never invited to join us. We watched gang members take over the street, a generational legacy never questioned and rarely relinquished, once observing a stabbing, the startling slash of blade against skin that split open like a wallet, blood pouring like hoarded valuables to the street, ducking back through the window as police sirens invaded the street and everyone scattered. We learned to smoke there, coughing like backfire from cars, trying again and again until we were triumphant. We pressed tightly against each other, wishing we could become a living organism too big to be defeated by the streets we knew and loved and dreaded.

We entered high school, examining our options, finding them non-existent, the myth of American accessibility just out of our reach making us feel dislocated, a subculture of a subculture. We needed a street not ours. Ours were constructs of white pustules of spit mingled with the rusty stains of blood like an offering to a malignant god. The only beauty we knew there were the splintered remnants of whisky bottles, prisms that captured the sun and refracted strange rainbows, the temporary white of sheets on clotheslines, waving like reluctant invitations to the pervasive soot. We found and claimed a street a quarter mile from us; it was our secret. The houses were a little nicer there, the sidewalk a little cleaner, the inhabitants better dressed; a street in a ghetto neighborhood that was one step up from our own.

"See you at The Street tonight," we whispered to each other when we passed in the high school halls, or at the handball court, or on the way to the grocery to buy milk or bread for our mothers. There was something precious, pristine about the street, as though it was on the upper east side, rather than in one of the most crime-ridden neighborhoods of Brooklyn. We created something through the power of imagination and desire, relishing a sense of freedom, of wildness, the illusion that we escaped, though nothing had changed at all. We were still always hungry, our bellies growling songs of *empty* until we stepped up what one of us called harvesting: surreptitiously pocketing bread, cheese, canned spaghetti, ravioli, tuna, salmon, soda, milk, candy. We became feral, eating with our hands, throwing food at each other, licking our fingers clean while adults passed with averted eyes. We were still always cold in our old jackets wrapped over tight sweaters, gloves with holes in the fingertips. We blew on our hands, stomped our feet, chased each other around the corner. We circled like a wagon train each night hoping for safety.

We played handball against the stoop or the walls, loud thumps that the residents complained about. The boys, grown taller, more muscular, made miraculous jumps onto the arms of street lamps then swung from them howling like Tarzan. The girls whispered with a new shy pride about having periods and stomach cramps, but especially about bad girls who did it, got pregnant and were expelled, while the boys who'd impregnated them bragged and suffered no consequences. Their stories were a warning mantra we repeated in rare acceptance of our mother's warnings the moment we began menstruating. That winter we huddled in the street's alleys, smoking, kissing, making the rounds incestuously from one to the other, experimenting, thrilled, and terrified. The knowledge of those girls who had vanished like fathers evading child support, girls as tarnished as any criminal, kept us on edge and cautious.

We snuck onto the subways daily, hovering by the turnstiles, listening for the deepening roar, feeling the vibrations in our feet, watching the light grow closer and brighter until it filled the tunnel. The doors of the graffitied cars would open, a giant mouth expelling people like dislodging pits, our signal to duck under the turnstiles and race in before the door closed. We visited new worlds: Coney Island with a white-capped ocean devoid of garbage or the East River's smells. People stripped, swam, sunbathed, their bodies glistening with suntan oil and salt water. They strolled the Boardwalk eating hotdogs, clouds of cotton candy, towering peaks of custard. We discovered the botanical gardens in Prospect Park with complex mazes and straight rows of flowers in blazing lush colors. We realized then the divergence of our puny green stalks whose flowers wilted even as they bloomed in vacant lots and through cracks in the sidewalk, that our poisoned air encouraged mutating to ensure survival. We went to Fulton Street, dazzled by an architecture of department stores and clean-windowed restaurants where consumers glutted themselves. The abundance of items, of affluence denied us was staggering, we wondered how we could share the same world and yet have nothing; we wondered why we had never been given a choice. Then we came home. We would always come home; it was our preordained destiny. We were certain we would always be together and today would echo into tomorrow and tomorrow and all the rest of the tomorrows with us trapped here. We slid into a pit of angry acceptance.

Here is how it changed for me. I went to the library, the only place warm enough in the winter, cool in the summer, a place of cushioned easy chairs occupying corners like hidden luxuries, sturdy scratched tables, and walls and walls of books. It was a small, three-room library, but to me it was a sanctuary with the silent, learned halls of the college I knew I could never attend. Only I went. I learned what existed beyond the borders of where we were.

One day, on my way home from the library, I passed a teenage mother pushing her stroller, her eyes dense with sleepiness, body going to fat, youth abandoning a prematurely defeated face. I watched her bend forward to replace the pacifier in her baby's mouth as he began crying, watched her straighten and stretch, hands on her lower back like a woman aging swiftly from eighteen to eighty. Something tightened in my body, a coil of fury and defiance and determination. I would not be trapped by an accident of birth. My Russian-Jewish grandparents escaped the shtetls, fled the "old country" to avoid being slaughtered. They went into exile to save themselves, fled with thousands of others in a Diaspora of desperation. I would go into exile as my ancestors did, my own, private Diaspora. I would create a new geography, locate a map of unknown roads, assume a new identity. I would focus, I must leave the street;

what had sustained me as a child was a prison in adulthood.

As in all Diasporas, the trailing threads of connection were severed. There are fragments of stories that can't be substantiated: Vietnam, drugs, teaching, dead in a traffic accident. But here I am in an airy, sunlit, whitewashed house whose open windows capture air scented by rose hips and ocean. Pottery lines the walls, earthy browns and pale porcelain celadon with delicate engravings, hand-sculpted pitchers of brilliant color. I sleep beside a husband who has never vanished. I wear a woven shawl of turquoise and purple, blouses of organic cotton in ancient colors, wool coats in winter. My friends have never stolen a candy bar, worn hand-me-downs of unbecoming colors, in sizes that don't fit, circumvented certain streets to insure safety. This is my life now, yet everything remains refracted by the streets: dark corners always suspect, certain sounds a warning, doors you must never turn your back on. The streets would not let go. I went back, finally, for an exorcism because an escape thirty-five years earlier was not enough.

My streets weren't there. These streets were prosperous with little boutiques, sidewalk vendors selling jewelry and second-hand books, expensive restaurants with clever names, shops with coffee that cost more than one of my mother's meals. There were condos, penthouses, studios with fine carpeting and walls of windows that looked out onto the city on the other side of the bridge and there was no differentiation. This was not a place I belonged. I walked these streets displaced again, as though I was in another country. I thought of the other five, wanted to be tele-pathic, desperately wanted to tell them, *we are the stuff of nearly forgotten myth, an early indigenous people whose homes have been demolished and land stolen; our landscape has been altered, made chic. We are an irrelevant past in this extension of a city we once thought unattainable.*

But those streets are not gone: they exist. I resurrect them in my dreams most nights, run wild on them, hide in the alleys while the filtered moonlight cast shadows of a past which can never really be left behind. There is an internal geography, a geography of the mind that under certain circumstances blurs the distinctions between then and now; I marvel at how after all this time and distance I am still a street kid, and still arrogant about it.

Country of the Past

My husband Kevin and I drift along the Finnish-Russian border as though suspended on the edge of a dream, my dream of Russia, or perhaps my mother's or grandparents' - the dream's architecture designed by immigrants burdened with want, dreams entangled with folkloric memory.

We ramble about in cool summer wind, time inexplicably permeable, food, smells, faces, all passports to the country of the past. The boreal forest of Ilomantsi is a construct of white, green, brown: birch, pine, spruce, larch, cedar, some oak for good measure. Dachas appear like roadside shrines beside the overgrown lakeside.

"Russia merely twenty kilometers from here," the Finns tell us when we stop for petrol. "You know Russia?" they ask. "So much trouble to go to, so much trouble to leave." They shrug again.

Indeed, we were told when first planning this trip after an invitation for Kevin to speak in Lapland that visas were particularly difficult to acquire right now.

So close this dream; so far.

"There's a way through the forest where you are no longer in Finland but in Russia." They point to tree-darkened depth, the lofty canopy, the chaga fungi spotting the rough brown bark like clumped charcoal, the shadowed path you can't see.

"Every year, picking berries and mushrooms, Finns wander into Russia, Russians into Finland."

"You want to go to Russia?" They laugh. "Too hard to get visa; have instead a bowl of kasha, maybe with some spring onions."

We pass signs in Finnish echoed by Cyrillic beneath, curves and lines like mysterious symbols. Here somewhere my grandparents fled Russia, traveled the path to the mountains, my grandmother's wooden bowl cradling the last of the Karelian pies and wrapped inside a ragged babushka of faded red and gold flowers, my grandfather tugging the hand of my seven-year old mother while her sister rode in a sling on his shoulders. How much snow then? How cold? What shoes? What coats?

It doesn't matter.

What's a little snow? A little cold? Worn boots?

Here somewhere on the other side of the border they stuffed hay into their shoes to absorb moisture and warm their feet. Somewhere else they found the boat to take them over the water to another somewhere else that would lead to different mountains and then, at the next somewhere else, another path to yet another border to yet another alphabet, to yet another ship to the Lower East Side of New York, where everyone it seemed spoke Russian and played sidewalk baseball.

But then, how else would a Jew in 1920 flee Russia?

We sit on the fire escape, my mother tending her plants. Her hair is covered with a babushka, her arms brown from the sun, her flowered housedress sprinkled with rich loam. The Russian station at the farthest end of the radio dial plays some lonesome song of violins and minor keys and a woman's voice filled with longing while my brother sleeps in the summer heat. I'm ten, examining a page in the textbook from my geography class. Russia is big; it swallows the page, swallows every country around it, swallows those same borders my grandparents crept over.

"Where Mama?" I ask yet again, pointing to the map. "Where were you born?"

"I told you. A shtetl in Russia."

"But where was the shtetl? Tell me the story."

"That is the story. The story is the shtetl. The story is Russia. The story is leaving Russia. The story is my two American children."

The song ends and a man's raspy voice announces something; he chuckles, then there's static, then another song.

My mother smiles and shakes her head

"What did he say?" I ask.

"He says they don't play this song any more in Russia; too many lines about freedom," she answers and loosens the dirt around a pot of pansies with a fork.

Her lips smile, but her eyes are sad. I look down at the map of Russia and feel a strange tug inside me.

"Should we try to get across the border?" my husband asks, pointing to a sign that says thirty kilometers to Kostomuksha.

He takes my silence as assent.

The sky is blue, gulls circling like children's kites, the summer air crisp with the last of the newly melted snow. The road ahead of us twists, curls around a rotary, a curve in the story of my life, then we cross a line distinct as a border, asphalt turns to dirt pockmarked by sharp stones, then finally thick mud, our rental car small and complaining and refusing to make the journey. Russia is thirty kilometers and a whole lifetime too far.

Would I recognize Russia? Would it be familiar? When we arrive at the border would I see some faint ectoplasm of my grandparents determinedly making their way to the freedom of forbidden Russian songs?

We turn, stop instead at a tiny store and buy a Karelian pie, a small fragrant furnace in our hands. What we can hold of Russia is butter dripping down our fingers.

"What we brought is what we could carry in our hands and on our backs" my mother says, pointing to her wooden bowl, the past scarring it with the deep wounds of the chopping knife, fresh American fruit covering the remnants of Russia, but not quite. And in the corner of her bedroom the scarf, so faded it tells only the story of time passing. Ah, but she's wrong, that's not all she brought; the rest is invisible except in unguarded moments when I see in her eyes the longing for forests turned crystal with ice, and the sun burning orange in the mirror of the Volga River, and the Caucasus mountains gone green and lush, fertile with berries.

Butter drips down my fingers, and the smell of it is drenched in nostalgia, and I am homesick now for this place I've never been.

Murmansk/Mypmahck the sign on the rotary announces. We are leaving Sodankyla, going to Rovaniemi, and the sign offers an alternative, forty kilometers to Russia, to Murmansk/Mypmahck; merely turn to the right, so easy, yes? We're eating cabbage strudel; who remembered how sweet the strudel, how good, the rich pastry rolled just so.

"This is what you ate as a child," my Anglo-American husband says in wonder and takes another bite.

He pauses at the sign, turns to me, asks, "Should we try again?"

And what would be our incredulous greeting if we arrived at the border without papers; *You come to Mypmahck without a visa? Without permission? Without a guide? For what purpose?*

What would we see if we craned our necks over the border crossing, past the guards, into the forest? Would we see the synagogue, the one so far north it's the last stop for Jews before they fall into the Baltic Sea?

I shake my head and he drives past.

Eat instead this delicious kugel from the Russian bakery

in Sodankyla where the woman with ruddy cheeks and full breasts and hair hidden under the old woolen scarf looked at my face and recognized my grandmother and spoke to me in Russian. It is becoming, and becoming, and becoming again that this language I never learned I almost remember. The words hide on my tongue like playful children. Listen hard, listen carefully, I can almost understand it; the syllables and vowels and inflections rearrange themselves in my head, a jigsaw puzzle fitting itself together to form some inscrutable sentence.

But there is more. Finland is a multicultural country after all, everyone following the brief summer and the twenty-four-hour brightness, the sun curving off the fields leaving just enough warmth to dispel winter. Each day now I spin in a kaleidoscope of languages, each linguistic lens of the same word different. In each city we pass through each nationality divines their own meaning from a single sentence, then the laughter, the explanations, this is like home, yes? Back home, in the New York of the 1930's and 40's and 50's; they brought to the tenements those languages and explanations and jokes, with the bowls and the candlesticks and the babushkas and the worn little books and the few photographs and the stories of Diaspora: Lithuanians, Poles, Ukrainians, Russians, Bulgarians, a pushcart of countries wheeling boisterously down the street.

This is what happens when traveling the border of Russia, I enter the country of the past. This morning in the mirror was my mother's eyes and then, like falling through a tunnel of time, my grandmother's and her grandmother's and then the grandmother before that and for the first time, I have met everyone – so pleased to make your acquaintance, have a blintz, have please a glass tea, sugar cube to rest between your teeth? Eat a little, then a little more.

In the shop in Petkeljarven in Finland, not to be confused please with Petrozavodsk in Russia, the Russian shop owner wears a suit, shirt, tie, all a little worn, all perfectly tailored – who is your tailor please to tell. He offers us "a glass tea." He holds out a plate of vareniki. "Please to have two, my wife's specialty."

The pastry is poignant with memory; fat little envelopes of my childhood come to rest temporarily in the here and now. He watches us, smiles. When we're done, the last crumbs finished, the "glass tea" empty, the plates and glasses and napkins whisked off to who knows where - "So now business." He turns to the glass cabinet behind him. With drama, with the air of a man exhibiting his most precious belongings, he removes two matryoshka. Their painted faces observe us serenely, denying the turmoil of their homeland. He opens the series of nesting dolls, lifts them out one by one from their fitted places like revealing carefully considered thoughts, and lines up on the counter these rows of lacquered icons.

"From before the revolution," he says. "Such quality, today such quality is not available. Today Russia is ruled by…" He stumbles for a word and finds a particularly American one; "By hooligans." He shakes his head and sighs.

"Cossacks," the old man upstairs said. "Russia was ruled by Cossacks. You lowered your eyes, you made your body small when you passed; your greatest aspiration was to get through a day without a kick." He shrugs.

It's the middle of summer; the blistering stale wind from the East River invades the neighborhood. I'm on my fire escape and he's on his. I lean back and crane my neck to see him. He sits at the edge of the ladder, feet dangling, looks down at me. He's old, forelocks tucked behind his ears, yarmulke a little askew, clothes a little shabby, but ah the tailoring of his shirt, of his pants, impeccable; this is workmanship, this is the workmanship of the old country, not available except in certain shops, hidden down side streets, shadowy places without signs that only a few know, affordable to only those few. The haze of the day imparts a dreamy quality to our exchange. I want him to tell me the things my mother won't – so Cossacks, a beginning, yes?

"Where are you from Mr. Palatnik?"

"Where?" he's startled. "From the shtetl, where else?"

"But which shtetl, where was it?"

"In Russia; where else? You think I'm Polish maybe, or Ukrainian?" He shakes his head.

"Where in Russia, Mr. Palatnik?"

"This matters, for why?"

This is familiar…too familiar.

"Did you know my mother in the shtetl?" I try another track.

He looks at me in astonishment then laughs. "My dear little girl, Russia is big country, from north to south, from east to west. How might I have met your mother, please to tell me?" His eyes are very humorous, very patient, very tired, filled with longing.

"You miss Russia, Mr. Palatnik?"

"What's to miss, the kicks, the curses, the stealing of your property?" He sighs. "Yes, I miss."

"Where in Russia are these from?" I ask the shop keeper.

"These?" He strokes them, touches them lovingly, caressing his children; "Naturally from Serviev Posad."

That is where the most expensive and finest and oldest are from. I know instantly he's lying. His eyes are without guile, his face empty of deceit, his voice sincere, the look of an honest man.

He asks an impossible price, waits for us to bargain. We surprise him and turn to leave. This is what I haven't inherited and what Kevin never owned; this love of bargaining.

We reach the door and he runs after us, grabs my husband's hand and puts something into it; a business card.

"Here on this card is my email. Anything you want, anything Russian, you email, I find it; anything. Good price too."

Desperation, didn't we escape desperation? I think. Didn't we leave the ghetto, the shtetl, the pogrom?
He hangs onto to Kevin's arm until Kevin nods quietly. "Yes, thank you."

We leave. We stand outside the store and look at each other.

"Let's get something to eat," my husband says.

"Potato piorgi from the Russian vendor in the food market," I suggest and he nods.

The food market extends for streets and streets and more streets: food, crafts, clothes, musicians, but mostly food. This food market; it shimmers in the sun like a busy mirage, the sheer noise of it rising all around us, it is color itself, a rainbow swirling through the streets in a dance of pleasure. The grass is littered with people eating ice cream or lunch or fruit, drinking beer or water or even, hidden a little in a bag for the sake of discretion although nobody cares, vodka or other spirits, clear and icy. Such noise, such joviality, such a feast, such a celebration of life, yes? Such accordion players, so good like you've never heard anywhere else, such melody.

"Have a second piorgi, what could it hurt; eat, eat up."

And I do, with greed, with gusto, wanting more even as my stomach hurts and why not; this is the manna of my childhood, this is my inheritance, my own little piece of the collective unconscious. Something is completing itself in me; I'm assuming my mother's loss; I'm ready to sing Korobeniniki, that old love song about a peddler and girl, except…except, I could never learn the words; the song always sung so fast, but also with such feeling, that I could get, yes, the meaning, so the words are irrelevant. This song is a fairy tale after all; a Russian fairy tale so of course a tragic ending.

"Like a fairy tale," the old, nearly-blind woman in the apartment next door tells me. How long has she been living here? How many mountains, how many ships, how many borders, how many languages to escape to this run-down tenement with its smell of decay and desolation, its gangs running rampant on the street like Cossacks.

"I've come to leave potato latkes my mother made."

"Сидеть, сидеть, sit, sit" she says in Russian.

I sit in the old chair with the cracked plastic seat. Her kitchen is a cave, the walls around the stove smudged dark from matches; I see in those smudges secret Cyrillic dreams from some ancient time.

"The palace outside St. Petersburg, mid-summer's eve, such a party." she says.

She smiles, her blind eyes watching something I'll never see.

"The palace, so lit up, so many lights, too many to count, brighter than the stars." She nods with pleasure. For one fleeting moment I see the child enchanted by the lights, the jewels and dresses on the women, the uniforms just so, always proper, such fabric, such tailoring. She watches out the kitchen door while her mother, a cook in the court of the czar, hurriedly piles caviar on plates, slices white fish, fills crystal decanters.

"Here, taste," her mother tells her and puts in her mouth a little white fish, a little caviar on slice bread, even the tiniest taste of cognac. "Who's to know, there's so much here," her mother says, all the while looking out at a guard who winks at the little girl; who's to know; eat a little and a little more.

"Swans and bears and reindeer carved from ice; giant ice statues, fire from bonfires shining on them," the old blind woman tells me.

I see the hot orange flames rising, casting flickering shadows so the ice sculptures are animated, alive, eyes glittering with the joy of being the center of attention, oblivious to the slow melt of their limbs. I see the platters, endless platters, silver, only the best please, the laughing, the dancing, the music thick as fog. The bonfires lighting it all before that world went up in flames, trampled under the boots and the promises and the lies.

I tiptoe out, leave the old woman with her mother's kindness, with the festivity, with the lingering taste in her mouth of caviar and white fish and rum cake; leave her trespassing into the country of the past while the country of today is busy going about its business.

But even then, at her door, I hold it open, hand on the doorknob, wondering if there is a way to slip through the cracks of her memory and into her world, bypass the fissures of passing time that dominate our lives and move beyond them into the blind woman's Russia which she keeps alive even as bits of it vanish with each refugee's death, flames of memory snuffed out like blowing out candles at the Czar's party till it is only a page in a history book.

But none of us can return to the past, especially one not ours, except in dreams and memories and sometimes in madness.

The fair is to celebrate Mid-Summer's Eve. We happen upon it while wandering the streets like nomads, admiring the architecture, the curving roofs and carved owls and sense of antiquity. We turn the corner and suddenly there is a quality to the air, such a festive blaze of joy; twenty-four hours of sunlight crowding out the darkness. Clouds dance in the sky with gratitude for the light that embraces the city with the promise of a few weeks more. The fair is flooded with people so dense we can scarcely move, all going about

the business of celebration. We are in the thickness of crowds and the smell of perfume and perspiration and beer, but also the competing scents of fresh bread and salmon and roasting meat and thick soups and pastries so flakey and sweet with summer fruit you could weep with joy.
Such a gift.

I try on enameled necklaces, admire woven shawls, run my fingers over silver candlesticks, sip a tiny taste of clear spirits so strong I cough as it hits my throat to the delight of the Finn who brews it. Kevin, always the scientist, wanders from stall to stall to count the tree rings in wooden platters and cups and cutting boards sanded to satin perfection, to examine the obvious wounding and infections of the trees that create such beautiful patterns, to compare it to those at home, to note the universality of everything. The vendors whose stalls we stop at are hopeful, the economy is bad after all and this is a hard way to earn a living, but when we shake our heads after admiring their products, they smile and say, "Enjoy the sunlight and the holiday and the city."
And then drifting over me – Korobeniniki played on a violin with the nearly too-much passion of a legendary melodrama; radio waves from a long ago Russian station beaming a siren song into this tiny bit of universe. Will I turn and see my mother nodding, eyes filled with desire for what once was?

I'm in a hypnotic trance, called home to a complex layering of continents and countries and cities bonded by the dispossessed's need for once more please to see my childhood.

It's a café in a little tent, sun shining through the white canvas, diffuse light illuminating people crowded around little tables filled with borscht and sorrel soup, fish and glasses of tea and an array of desserts so laden with memory I can barely breathe. There is a menu in Russian, but it's not necessary; the food is its own explanation. At the entrance to the tent is an accordion player, a man with a balalaika, but most lively, a violin player in his fifties, eyes filled with mischief as he warms the crowd with a new and lively song. Children dance in front of the tent, the swirling and kicking and bending of intuition; the special gift of the young who obey the desire to move and who understand that all of it is grace.

The violin player has closed his eyes, his face wistful, his mouth tinged with sorrow, the notes are so sweet, so reminiscent that the world falls away and there is only this little tent, and the children dancing. I am a matryoshka, my years in America being lifted off one by one till all that remains is something I experience through instinct. The country of the past shimmers like a mirage I can almost touch and there is the promise that for a few moments I can reverse the Diaspora, I can fulfill my mother's dream. I understand that my children will never experience what I feel. I am one of the last descendents of a very specific group of émigrés, the final bridge, the vanishing repository for their memories and the inheritance of this particular yearning.

Standing opposite me is an elegant woman in her eighties; such jewelry, such carefully coiffed hair, such tailoring of her simple skirt and blouse, and who please to tell me is your tailor? Her eyes are closed and she sways, cocooned by the music and the longing and her face mirrors my own and when she opens her eyes and sees me she recognizes that.

She nods at me before closing her eyes once again. I want to move closer, to take her hand, kiss her on both cheeks, so pleased to make your acquaintance, to exchange muttered feelings of condolences and desire, but there is no need to, we are joined by our mutual love and loss. The Russia of my mother's childhood, of the Lower East Side's childhood, of this elegant woman's childhood, have long vanished, and I will most likely never see what has replaced it, still I have temporarily come full-circle, crossed back over the rivers and mountains and the paths and borders to a wild and beautiful place left long-ago. I too will close my eyes and pretend that she and I have traversed generations and time and expulsions to stand together, though only briefly, in my dream besides the Volga River.

Hair

One Saturday a month, for twenty-five years, my mother and the upstairs neighbor Frances, dyed each other's hair. The two would chat and gossip over a growing mound of lipstick-tipped cigarettes and endless cups of coffee as they "partook of the fountain of youth," their euphemism for this process. They'd ruthlessly obliterate gray from furrowed rows with the determination of a farmer eliminating weeds. My mother was a practical woman, her hairstyle a boyish wash and wear, yet she continued this time-consuming process until she died at sixty-two. She insisted that although she was a "mere file clerk" her office demanded a youthful appearance because she was visible behind the stacks.

"You tell me," she said, admiring the "youth job" in the mirror. "When do you see a woman under ninety with gray hair."

I remember these Saturdays as bathed in sunlight regardless of weather, the women's faces flooded with laughter, purpose, and a too rare sense of relaxation. As single mothers trying to earn a living and keep house, they had few moments of rest, and even fewer for self-indulgence.

Hair-coloring fell midway between necessity and that self-indulgence. Frances was a devout Irish-Catholic and my mother an Eastern European Jew; what united them was the struggle to survive, concern about their children, and the perhaps universal women's dilemma of hair.

I shared that dilemma. Whenever I complained about my kinky hair, my mother shook her head. "When you were a baby, I couldn't keep you in the carriage." She inhaled deeply on her cigarette, her eyes sharply critical of my unhappiness and continued, "Strangers would grab you up they were so in love with your platinum curls. Women would kill for your hair. You don't know how lucky you are." She'd shake her head again, disappointed in her foolish daughter.

As a girl of eight or nine, I strove to remember when my hair was an asset rather than a liability. I closed my eyes imagining bright wisps of curls haloed charmingly around my small child's face. I sometimes manufactured bits of comforting memory in counterpoint to attending a school mostly populated by Irish students with shining straight hair. My hair and my Jewishness had had relegated me to the ranks of "the other."

My fuzzy hair, even at that young age, seemed symbolic of an inability to fit in, an outward manifestation of my internal shy awkwardness and feelings of inadequacy. Further, it suggested something outside of the realm of acceptability, an inability to conform to the mores of the day. Taunts of poodle-pup, coupled with little barks, trailed me down school corridors, but in a school beset by gangs, stealing and truancy, name-calling was a minor problem ignored by school authorities. Each morning when my mother wet and detangled my hair with a wide-toothed comb, I complained, cried, begged not to go to school. She always shook her head, reminding me that "an education is the most important thing you can get and it's free."

By junior high school, I discovered that I didn't need my mother's permission and became a visitor rather than student during much of my pre-college academic career, showing up periodically to walk from home room to first period class with Barry, a boy I had a crush on. Walking through the halls one day, he pointed to Alex, a sweet and lovely girl in our grade who wore her long blonde hair wrapped around her head.

"Isn't her hair beautiful!" Barry said.

I nodded, offering my best smile, glumly realizing that my hair would never look like the beauteous Alex's, and I would never inspire that kind of admiration.

Barry's remark led to me spending even more time in Manhattan at the big public library, Central Park, or one of the museums. One afternoon after emerging from the subway station, I walked a different route home through a predominantly Puerto-Rican neighborhood and spied a small beauty shop with a sign in English and Spanish that advertised expertise in cutting curly hair. The shop-window was clean and welcoming with advertisements for hair products and photos of beautiful woman with tamed hairstyles. I couldn't stop thinking about it and after I retrieved my brother from the baby-sitter, I impatiently paced our tiny apartment until my mother arrived. I harangued her for two days until she finally relented and gave me five dollars for a hair cut.

The next afternoon, five dollars scrunched down in my pocket, I walked into the empty beauty parlor. A young Hispanic woman named Lillian whose wavy hair suggested now vanquished curls ushered me into a chair then surveyed my head.

"I've never worked with hair so kinky," she confessed. "Not even my own."

I was silent, my chest painful.

"But I can do this fine," she said in a surge of confidence.

Lillian turned me away from the mirror in order to surprise me with my newly obedient locks when completed.

For some period of time hair fell around me like yellow snowflakes. Her face was tight with concentration, the snap of her scissors unnerving as she continued for what seemed like hours. When she was finished she stepped back to look at me. Her eyes announced failure. She silently turned me toward the mirror and I saw a stranger as shorn of hair as a new Marine. My face seemed huge, my forehead high as a balding man's, an androgynous specter I'd never met. I looked at her in helpless despair and she muttered apologies, looked away and said she wouldn't take any money.

"When it grows back," she said. "I'll do it for free."

That possibility didn't exist.

"I'm sorry," she whispered again after I gathered my courage to step out onto the street.

On the way home, blindly panic-stricken, I bumped into a man who put a kind hand on my shoulder and said, "Careful there son," adding to my humiliation.

That night, after quietly surveying me, my mother said, "It will grow back before you know it."

My marine cut further infused me with a sense of worthlessness, unmitigated by my mother's continuing reassurance it would grow back, that it allowed my beautiful features to show, that I was not my hair and my worth was not judged by how long or curly or blonde it was. I finally said that if that was really true she wouldn't dye her own hair.

She looked at me thoughtfully and lit a cigarette before answering. "In the business world women need to look young. It doesn't matter how old you are, you need to look like a chick or they don't hire you."

Her response silenced me, suggesting, as it did, years to come in my struggle with hair.

In junior high school I discovered orange juice cans to attain the sleek hairstyles of Grace Kelley, Audrey Hepburn, Kim Novak. In what would become a nightly ritual I gathered together long hairpins, a wide-toothed comb, a jar of warm water, and clean cans. I stood before the little mirror over our kitchen sink, dipped the comb into the jar, wound a small section of hair so tightly around a can that my head hurt, then fastened it with hairpins. When the pinning was complete and copious amounts of hair spray applied, my hair, which resembled something destined for the trashcan, was covered with an enormous kerchief. Interestingly enough, a popular style evolved from this, and the streets were often filled with adolescent girls wearing kerchiefs over hair rollers like badges of femininity.

The sleepless discomfort of my head never actually resting

on the pillow, of sharply-poking pins gone astray, punctuated by my mother's incredulity about it, were offset by an imagined sense of being fashionable, that is if it didn't rain allowing my petrified helmet to retain its shape. My lacquer-stiffened hair, when I looked in the mirror most mornings, seemed a promise of new possibilities - through discomfort and hard work I could achieve some measure of acceptance and a small circle of friends. My assumptions were wrong; a history of being an outcast coupled with my lack of school attendance and being a Jew, guaranteed the continuity of my status.

Despite my continuing absences I was promoted to high school because I managed to pass all my exams, showing up to take them, then leaving, mostly spending time at the New York Public Library, which I'd fallen in love with. The beautiful, light-filled reading room of elegant wooden chairs and long tables, couched in silence, literacy and contemplation, housed more than a few eccentrics and provided a place where I felt I belonged, a belief fostered by the solitary nature of others. Here I pursued my own interests, studying many obscure books while surreptitiously sweeping flakes of hair spray that resembled dandruff from the open pages. It was while sitting outside on the wide stone steps waiting for the library to open that I overheard a conversation between two African-American girls. They were rhapsodizing about a beauty parlor called Straight-Shot. I turned to look at them. Both girls, a bit older than me, had pin-straight hair. As soon as the library opened, I raced to the Manhattan telephone book, and located the Midtown beauty salon.

That afternoon I made an appointment. My mother,

beleaguered by my continuing unhappiness about my hair, agreed to give me twenty-five dollars, a fortune to wrangle from her budget. That summer I could get working papers and I assured her that if the treatment was successful I would pay for it out of my earnings.

"You'll have to," she said. "I can't afford this."

"I know," I told her. "Thanks Ma and if it works maybe everything will change."

She shook her head and said, "Your hair is beautiful, one day you'll believe that."

"Maybe one day, Ma. But not today." I hugged her with gratitude.

That Saturday morning, I walked into an enormous room more a warehouse than a beauty saloon. The air reeked with lye, burnt hair, and stale conditioner. There were at least twenty-five black women standing behind chairs so crowded together they barely had room to work and large hair-dryers stationed anywhere there was room. Straight-Shot was owned by a thin Caucasian man in an expensive suit who checked appointment times when a customer walked in the door. Against one wall was a private station occupied by the owner's brother, Mr. Sam. Mr. Sam had an enormous mirror, a desk of various implements, a cushy barber's chair, and his own hair dryer.

It was immediately apparent that white girls were assigned to Mr. Sam, while black girls were assigned to whichever woman's chair became free. This made for a faster flow for the black woman, and I indicated that I wanted to be styled by one of them. The owner instead sent me to a small row of seats telling me I was next for Mr. Sam whose appointments were spaced out. As I waited, I really understood for the first time the meaning of segregation, something I'd never noticed in New York where so many different nationalities and skin shades crammed the streets together. It suddenly, really hit me that the black kids in school sat at their own table and walked home together, something so taken for granted I'd never thought about it before. In many ways, I had more in common with these students yet the possibility of a friendship hadn't occurred to me. As I sat there I noted a snobbishness emanating from Mr. Sam and the white girls, all better-dressed than I was, and the working-class consciousness instilled in me by my socialist mother spurred my anger. I stood to insist on one of the black women, but at that moment Mr. Sam motioned that it was my turn and I was far too eager for straight hair to protest.

The process consisted of a thick lye-scented paste combed on, duration carefully timed to avoid destroying the hair and to only minimally burn the scalp. It went quickly, girls were moved to the sink, paste washed out, conditioner applied, hair set on enormous rollers and dried.

The room was overpoweringly noisy and seemingly chaotic, but in truth it was orderly. The black women knew exactly what they were doing and turned out head after head of shining flips, the popular hairstyle of the moment. In contrast, Mr. Sam applied the paste, took his client to the sink where a black woman washed her hair, set it in rollers and placed her under the hair dryer, pulled out the rollers when the hair was dry. Mr. Sam took it from there, lingering over each head, moving a lock of hair just so, then with a "voila" and showy flourish of hands perhaps similar to that of a doctor after brain surgery, sent her on her way. After this first time I insisted on being processed by one of the black women and the astonished owner shrugged his shoulders, and assigned me to whoever was available.

But that first time; I left Straight-Shot trailed by the odor of lye, my scalp on fire, my eyes red from fumes, but with gloriously straight hair. My mother wrinkled up her nose at the putrid smell and my brother ran around the kitchen holding his nose.

"I liked your curls," my mother said.

"You didn't have to live with them," I answered.

"If it makes you happy." She shrugged.

"I'm happy."

Thus began my fifteen year relationship with Straight-Shot. By that summer I had working papers and a job and paid for my every-two-months appointment. I did indeed develop a small circle of friends, most probably due to my new-found confidence and more frequent appearances in school. That Monday, after my first appointment, attending school to take a test, I approached the black students' table hesitantly. They looked up at me with startled concern. The civil rights movement was a faint whisper and I realized that I had no models of black/white friendships to guide me, that would come with my first adult job when I developed an integrated circle of friends and participated in civil rights marches, but then I felt intimidated by my own ignorance. I realized that the vague thread I might have begun a friendship on, kinky hair, no longer existed. I nodded, smiled, and walked to my own table.

By the time I graduated and got my first adult job straight hair was a way of life. In between appointments, and whenever it rained, I used my mother's iron, on a low setting, to smooth my hair. Bits of spray starch, transferred from iron to hair, sometimes fell during work or on a date and embarrassed me, but the cost, burning scalp, one-week of putrid odor, and periodic ironing felt worth it.

My first husband, who was Cuban, loved my hair. By the time we married I had grown it quite long and often wore it in braids. He felt the putrid odor a small price to pay for my appearance. Over the next few years we had two sons and moved to Long Island. I continued my trips into the city to get my hair straightened. Despite the shifting culture around it, the civil rights movement, the women's movement, the Vietnam war, Straight-Shot never changed. Walking into the room was walking into the past. Mr. Sam, on his platform, never grayed despite being at least sixty. It was clear from his comb-over that he was balding. By then some black women were shifting to afro's and Straight-Shot didn't have the same mob scene. It had settled into a kind of placid conservatism that seemed reminiscent of those country clubs and lounges cradled by the past that men went to in order to escape the emerging present.

I had formed a close friendship with Donna, a black woman I worked with on the library board and in a group to establish a women's shelter for battered women. We spoke about many things: anti-Semitism, racism, poverty in America and, one afternoon, hair. Both Donna and I had processed hair, and I spoke about letting mine go natural, noting how many white women in the civil rights movement had hair as kinky as their African-American friends.

It was an interesting time to be "the other," for we were now in groups, a new kind of conformity marking us, moving us, in one sense, further away from our original, outcast designation into what was becoming an in-group. A romantic notion of being the outsider, personified by films like Easy Rider and Billy Jack, began to creep into the culture. The clothing, beards, hair-styles, idioms, vernacular were slowly being assimilated into the population at large, diminishing their initial rebellious inference, and although few actually engaged in civil disobedience, many had acquired the "uniform." I realized that in this environment it took less courage to allow my hair to revert to type. I asked Donna if she thought about it.

"Well," she answered. "Even with kinky hair, you pass for white so to speak, not me. I'm not ready, it's a little scary, we're still too close to slavery, Jim Crow and lynching, and look at what's happening in the south. It would also be a problem with my part-time job if I showed up with an Afro."

"I'm sorry," I whispered.

She shook herself, then smiled and hugged me. "You should be sorry - all those Jews killing Jesus."

We laughed then, although none of it was funny, merely absurd and entrenched.

Over the next six months my hair grew out. It was a weird mix of long, straight pipes of hair narrowing into tightly curled wire. When there was enough of that wire I cut off everything that was straight. My husband was furious and insisted I straighten it again; I refused. He then bought a long blonde wig and insisted that I wear it out with him; I refused again. My decision to attend college, help establish a women's center and run consciousness-raising groups with a feminist therapist, contributed to the disintegration of my marriage. My curly hair became an outward reflection of what I felt inside; a growing confidence and determination.

One afternoon, when Donna and I were handing out leaflets to establish a traveling library, I told her about the problem with my husband. She was sympathetic but had no suggestions. I held out a leaflet to a man in a business suit hurriedly passing by and he glared, actually shoved me and shouted, "Damn Kikes and Niggers everywhere forcing things down your throat."

Donna and I looked at each other and she said, "Girl, guess you don't pass for white after all; that nappy head gave you away."

This time I felt a sense of pride and Donna said that for the first time she was seriously thinking about letting her hair go natural.

Donna moved to Seattle a few years later and we lost touch with each other. By then I had grown more politically active and my husband, a decent man mired in a chauvinistic culture, couldn't accept the changes in me. We divorced. Soon after I graduated, my mother died, and my children and I moved to Maine near a close friend and her children.

One winter morning, five years later, I woke in my empty

bed to snow falling outside and I realized how lonely Maine can be in the winter no matter how many friends. I looked at myself in the mirror as I brushed my teeth and realized that my tight, mop of hair was now more gray than blonde. I thought about growing older alone, the prevalence of dyed hair among nearly all my friends, and my "business" presence, as my mother would have put it. Later that day, I had lunch with an unmarried friend whose electric-white hair was greatly admired. She smiled at my compliment that it looked beautiful with the blue dress she wore. After a moment or two, however she said, "All my friends love it, but I seem invisible to single men, and even when shopping, I have to really be assertive to get service. It's as though once your hair is white, you get placed into the category of anonymous gray-haired women. It seems like the only people who see me, not my hair, are my friends."

Her words, coupled with my loneliness, haunted me on the drive home.

"The hell with it," I said. I drove to the drugstore, found the closest shade I could to my natural color, drove home, took a deep breath and opened the bottles. Later, I stared in the mirror at the familiar blonde and felt I looked ten years younger. I shook my head and whispered, "Here I am, Ma; partaking of the fountain of youth."

My second husband, who I met a few months later and whose silver hair is considered distinguished, is ten years younger than me. For me, that fact justified dying my hair as routinely as visiting Straight-Shot once was. One evening, after I'd colored my hair that day, my husband came home from work, kissed me hello and looking at my hair said, "Once again no silver strands among the gold."

We laughed and then he added thoughtfully, "I hope you're not doing it for me. I really don't care."

"No," I assured him. "I'm doing it for myself." I wondered, however, if that was true; I was all too conscious of our ten years difference.

A few nights later, over dinner with my older son's family, my son hugged me Good-by and said, "You know Mom, it's weird to have a wife who is grayer than my mother."

On the way home, I thought about how comfortable my daughter-in-law was with her gray hair. She provided the role model for her daughters that I'd never had and I realized that if enough of us provided that type of role model, we might be able to change cultural perceptions. I remembered that old sixties adage; if you're not part of the solution, you're part of the problem.

"I'm going to go grey," I told Kevin solemnly, the words and my voice portentous, as though the decision was life-altering. For Pete's sake, I told myself, you're just letting your hair grow out.

I kept my hair short during the growing-out process, self-conscious as the gray pushed the blonde further and further from my face till I was neither one color or the other. More than once a woman in the supermarket or at a conference or dinner party said to me, "You're growing your hair out? When I nodded, I was often told, with a head-shake, "I wish I was brave enough to do it."

I wondered at the concept we shared that it was brave to

just let your hair revert to grey. I finally snapped at one woman, "For God's sake, I'm not racing into a burning building to rescue children, I'm just letting my hair grow out." She looked at me strangely.

Finally, one morning, the last remnants of blonde fell to the floor under the onslaught of my beautician's scissors. She had initially declared my face too youthful for gray, but when we saw the pure white curling around my head, she said, "It's gorgeous. Women would kill to have hair like that, thick and curly and that shade of silver."

I chuckled at the similarity with my mother's description of my curls, looked into the mirror and there my mother was as she might have looked had she stopped coloring her hair. I burst into tears, needing to immediately reassure my hairdresser that it had nothing to do with her.

For the most part, the difference my gray hair made was so small that I often forgot I'd let it grow out and was jolted when I spied myself in a mirror somewhere.

"Look at me," I joked to Kevin. "I'm finally growing older with you."

A year later Kevin and I went to Lapland, for him to present a week-long work study program for international students while I worked on a series of essays about the experience. I often went out to the ponds and woods with the working groups and helped take samples. It was arduous work that involved hauling logs, pushing through brush, wading through bogs; I had a blast. Most of the students were young women in their twenties, but it was easy to

63

strike up friendships with them, despite age and language. We discussed cultural differences between our varied countries, shared life experiences, and even had a discussion about Lyme Disease which I'd had for an extended period of time and which was epidemic in many of their countries. I felt accepted as an equal.

The final day there we had a feast, the cafeteria tables heavy and pungent with reindeer steaks, grilled vegetables for the few vegetarians and a plethora of sweets, including scrumptious Finnish chocolate. Many of the students celebrated by drinking heavily and joyously. Just before the party was over, Erica, the unofficial spokeswoman for the group, came up to me and with a hug said, "We girls always talk about you and we want to be just like you when we're your age."

I looked behind her at the young faces beaming at me while I thanked her for what she meant as a compliment. I'd thought of myself as one of them while we worked together never realizing they were acutely aware of my age every moment. They had relegated me to the defined category of older women rather than viewing me as an individual and were thus surprised that I didn't fit the stereotype. I lay in bed that night thinking about otherness in America, propagated by false assumptions, stereotypes that had a life of their own. I'd encountered it as a Jew, as having kinky hair, as being an early anti-war activist, and most recently as one of the aging. Only a year earlier nobody had ever used the term "your age" to describe me, merely because my hair was dyed; certainly my wrinkles were fully on display.

Her words, however, inspired an unexpected pang of

anxiety; no matter how active I was, I was still ten years older then my husband who was often surrounded by young women. Despite Kevin always being scrupulously faithful, complimentary and loving, the anxiety persisted.

The next day, when we arrived in Helsinki, I went into a drugstore, purchased hair coloring, and dyed my hair in the hotel room. When it was done I looked in the mirror and, indeed, I looked ten years younger. It hadn't changed anything physically, I was still a sixty-five year old woman, but what changed was the attitude of everyone around me; I was no longer a woman of "your age" indicative of an allowable suspension of belief about age that often occurs once a woman dyes her hair. Once again my hair was symbolic of societal beliefs.

Everyone was startled back home having assumed I was done with hair coloring. I felt cowardly at succumbing yet again to my fear of stereotypes, indeed accepting an insulting one to my husband, that men always seek younger women. I knew my effort to conceal the aging process would ultimately fail; that soon the difference between my hair color and face would present too great a denial of the obvious. Yet still I clung to my need for a certain kind of acceptance, even if that acceptance was based on cruel stereotypes about older woman.

I thought about my mother and Frances fifty years ago, helping one another to dye their hair at that cracked kitchen table. I wished that my mother were with me now, that I could put my arm around her and joke about the fountain of youth. I wished I could say, Listen, mom - let's be role models for your great-granddaughters and my grand-daughters and stop pretending we're still chicks when everyone knows we aren't. I imagined her, then, cradling my aging face between her hands and saying, why not, we'll do it together.

Rejection

For quite a while my husband and I lived on an obscure road in Maine with only one nearby house, glimpsed through our kitchen window. In summer that house was not visible, the thick canopy of oak and maple a living wall; by November, however, stark winter branches formed an empty frame around it. It was owned by a couple in their early forties who had an eleven-year-old son, Paul. Bob, an affable, graying man with a cherubic smile, welcomed us warmly the day we moved in, said he traveled a lot for work, something Kevin did as well, but to call on him when he was there if we needed anything. Lois, his wife, a slender attractive woman wearing a thick cardigan she pulled tightly around her body, walked across their lawn and directed a bright smile at Kevin, reaching for his hand and seconding Bob's offer of help. The warmth of her smile implied a possible friend or at least a casual acquaintance to share a walk or cup of coffee. When she turned to me, however, her eyes narrowed, she nodded briefly, then walked away.

Startled, I watched her retreating back, thanked Bob who didn't mention his wife's behavior, and retreated to my own house. Once inside, I looked at Kevin in confusion and asked, "What did I do?"

"What do you mean?" he asked.

"You couldn't have missed it. She was friendly to you, but didn't even smile at me."

He shrugged. "She was probably just in a hurry. Don't be sensitive."

But I am sensitive, and always have been, to the subtle clues people put out. I grew up in an anti-Semitic, violent ghetto neighborhood, and reading the clues accurately was essential.

"I don't think I'm wrong," I mumbled. "But I'll give her the benefit of the doubt."

Over the next few months it seemed clear to me that I'd been right. If Lois and I chanced to be in our back yards at the same time she'd swiftly move to the most distant corner to avoid any contact. Paul, a lanky, intelligent youngster with his dad's gentle smile, had on more than one occasion forgotten his house key and done homework over milk and cookies at my kitchen table. Once his mother's car appeared in their driveway he'd dash out the door with a quick thank-you as though warned not to linger once she returned. She never waved through her car window.

"She hates me," I'd tell Kevin. "And I don't know why."

"She doesn't hate you," he'd say. "She's probably just shy."

I didn't point out that she never seemed shy with him. Whenever I vacated the back yard, leaving Kevin alone to tend the garden or move snow depending upon season, Lois emerged from what seemed a sequestered avoidance of my presence, to stride briskly across the property line. I couldn't hear their conversation, but her face was animated, her body language lively, her head tossed back in laughter at something Kevin said. She'd furtively glance at our house as though watching for my appearance to time her escape. Three years after we'd moved in, she'd nodded hello to me perhaps five times while Kevin was full of information about her job, her childhood in Canada, her frequent visits home and to Bob's family in Florida.

"You just haven't caught her in the right mood," he offered, when I pointed this out.

"After this many years there should have been at least one right mood, and anyway it's not my responsibility to gauge her moods in order to have a neighborly conversation, or at least a few words, with her."

My voice was sharp, reflecting the frustration I felt after three winters of living there. There were days when I had no face-to-face conversation with anyone, the roads too hemmed in by snow for me to drive anywhere, days when the richness of life felt shallow and I feared that I'd forgotten how to converse. In warm weather our six acres of granite, wildlife and forest was wonderful. Friends visited to explore, eat and talk, and in the long, sunlight-lit days of summer, I visited them, driving to upstate Maine, New Hampshire, Massachusetts, but after the first snow a muffled silence surrounded me. My loneliness was intensified by Kevin's frequent trips, sometimes a week long, power outages and icy roads. I'd glance at our neighbor's house through the trees when I took a break from writing or reading to make a cup of tea in the kitchen and would remind myself, as resentment tightened my throat, not everyone had to like me. Still, I reasoned, she didn't even give me an opportunity to present a reason for her not to. I wasn't asking for much, a few moments of human interaction to dispel the isolation.

"I wish she'd at least give me a chance to prove I'm unlikable," I told Kevin one evening, after Lois had seen me emerge to collect my mail then scooted back to her house with her own, not even glancing in my direction.

"Maybe you've misjudged her; I still think she's shy," Kevin said, but with less conviction than previously shown.

I felt confirmation of her puzzling dislike of me toward the end of that third year. My son Carl, a singer-songwriter, had a concert in a nearby town and I threw a pre-concert potluck. I invited friends, but also my elusive neighbor, her husband and son, believing that the crowd would present an opportunity for her to avoid me in my own home while I observed her, trying to ascertain the reason for what I viewed as her almost pathological dislike of me. It didn't work. Although Bob and Paul came, Lois didn't. The food was good, the conversation lively, and Carl and his musician friends made an appearance and sang a few songs as prelude to what would come later in the concert hall. Bob and Paul spoke with nearly everyone, Paul enjoying his conversation with my close friend who was head of the English Department in the school he attended, Bob exchanging ideas with another salesman at the party.

"We had a great time, but won't be able to go to the concert," Bob said on the way out. "Lois isn't feeling well and asked us to come home after the potluck."

Paul blushed and didn't meet my eyes as he repeated his father's thanks for the evening.

"Well, I hope she feels better and I'm sorry she couldn't make it," I said, although I wanted to say, she missed a great time but she wasn't missed. I wanted Bob and Paul to go home and tell her how great our friends are, how delicious the food was, how enjoyable they found the music. I wanted them to tell her what a great hostess I was, making her question the wisdom of her avoidance of me. I wanted her to deeply regret not coming.

I was also disgusted with myself for feeling it important and for experiencing such resentment, a quality familiar from a childhood with few friends, and that I struggled against as an adult as something useless and self-destructive. I saw the childishness of my feelings, yet couldn't move past them.

In bed that night, Kevin no longer suggested it was all in my imagination. "Yeah," he said. "It seems as though she just doesn't like you."

"But why," I said. "What did I do?"

"You're a therapist," Kevin said. "How many times have you explained to me emotions aren't always rational. Besides, what do you care, you have friends who love you."

"I know I have friends," I said irritably. "The problem is that this house is far from them and anything else. It's not just her total rejection of me, but rather that there is nobody on the road to accept me. I don't want her to be my best friend; I'd just like her to say hello."

"So why are you angry with me?" he said, responding to my tone.

"I'm not angry with you," I snapped. "I'm not even angry with her. I'm angry with myself for letting it matter."

I tossed restlessly long after Kevin's breathing had quieted into a gentle confirmation of sleep. Why did it bother me so much? Why was her rejection so important? Why couldn't I shrug and just let it go? I thought of a close friend with a well-received first novel who quoted the oft-repeated cliché, that the review she remembered most was a highly critical one. In the same vein a friend, now happily engaged, couldn't let go of her desire to know why a man she'd dated a few times, and who she thought liked her, stopped calling.

Rejection, something both universal and utterly personal, was all too familiar. As one of the few Jews in our neighborhood I was made fun of, called names at best, and beaten up at worst. My teenage years of kinky hair and sharp features came ten years before the culture grew to consider them exotically attractive and I was dateless during adolescence, acquiring just a few friends in high school and feeling like a failure. It was the women's movement and college that raised my self-esteem. Lois' dislike of me, seemingly devoid of actual reasons, woke all those feelings of inadequacy never far below the surface. I thought ruefully about how the wounding we experience as children remain scabs, easily picked open. Kevin had often remarked that Lois and I had nothing in common, nothing we might build a friendship on. I was certain that he was right yet wanted her to offer friendship. I thought of something I'd once heard; "I always wanted to be invited to the party that I didn't want to go to."

Except, this was a party that I did want to go to; it almost felt as though my psychic survival depended on it. Each winter, the loneliness grew more and more acute till it often seemed the only emotion I had. The absence of others was a giant presence, silence the loudest sound in my world, my friendships reduced to an abstraction with contact only through emails or telephone calls and those subject to the vagaries of weather and the electric company. Some mornings when I walked or snow-shoed past Lois' house I thought that the occasional cup of coffee, or even a smile, could make all the difference in my life.

You carry your solitude within, I reminded myself; we all do. But solitude was an iffy thing. Growing up in New York one could be friendless, but didn't have to be isolated. The twenty-five cents my mother gave me provided a devil dog and hot chocolate at the local Five and Dime where the woman behind the counter got used to seeing me and would ask about school, my mother, my brother. I could wander the corridors of the many museums or the big public library. Even walking the streets, jostled by crowds, listening to the tail ends of conversations, provided company. Unlike this little rural road in Maine, you could step outside your door and there would be people.

The therapy books I'd read when I was a practicing psychotherapist indicated that loneliness and isolation often led to a deep depression. I felt myself the proof; despite writing, a profession I love, reading wonderful books, and living in a place of great beauty, by mid-winter I struggled to get out of bed each morning.

The last winter we lived there was one of the worst; blizzards narrowed the roads, power outages were frequent,

Kevin was often stranded in another state. Paul, who'd been good for a smile, was away in college and Bob, who I'd seen rarely anyway, traveled constantly. While friends invited me to stay overnight at their homes, the storms were so frequent it seemed futile to go and then come home to yet another white-out. I felt myself the only person in a vast expanse of pines, boulders and ten-foot snow mountains. I began to lose my sense of self: was I intelligent? Interesting? Humorous? Good company? If a friend laughs with you, nods when you say something, engages in a discussion or even an argument, it reinforces a sense of your importance to somebody else. I realized, as I often did, how much our concept of self depends upon what others reflect back to us. Lois, the only available mirror, assumed ridiculous importance and the fact that she mirrored dismissive dislike made me doubt my likeability or relevance. I waited for weekends when Kevin was home or when friends, who worked in more traditional jobs, braved the roads and visited; still, I was such a long distance from anything that by mid-winter I had almost no visitors. These times with friends couldn't fill the growing hole I experienced. I began to imagine that Lois had discovered something foul and unacceptable about me that nobody else saw. I began to revisit everything I'd ever done that I regretted, everything that had ever brought me shame: irritability with my children, the friend whose secret I'd shared with another, the woman whose husband I'd flirted with, hateful retorts toward my first husband during the disintegration of our marriage, lying to my mother as a teen-ager, all reinforced my unacceptability and discounted anything good about me.

I woke each morning with a sense of dread and shame at all the things I'd done, including those I couldn't remember.

As that winter slowly passed, each day somehow longer than twenty-four hours, it became an almost moral imperative, an act of redemption for any past transgressions, for Lois to acknowledge me; to say hello, to engage at least superficially. It almost resembled the single-minded desperation of a captive striving to have his jailor acknowledge his humanity; I recognized something obsessive about it, but somehow every slight, every dismissive glance, every anti-Semitic joke, every boy who'd ever poked fun at me, had coalesced into the massive burden of Lois' rejection.

Achieving her acknowledgement became one of my daily goals, along with the amount of words written, and the meals prepared. I devised my strategy and followed through on it. If I saw her, I would quickly step outside, wave hello, ask how she was, shouting my greeting if she was at the furthest end of her property. She had only two choices, to totally ignore me or to at least return my hello; she chose to answer with the fewest words possible, never inquiring how I was. I felt victorious in some small regard that this was the first step; I never got an opportunity to take it one step further.

One Sunday afternoon Paul knocked on our door. We greeted him with a smile, a question about college, invited him in, but he stood outside our door awkwardly then blurted out, "My dad died yesterday."

His eyes filled with tears and he continued, "My mom wanted you to know that she's alone now. She's over at the funeral home."

We were silent with sad surprise. Paul explained in a choked voice that his dad had been sick with a degenerative disease for a long time, but that they'd imagined he'd have a few more years.

"Paul, we're so very, very sorry. Your dad was a great guy; always warm and joking with a friendly smile for everyone," I said.

"Yeah," he answered. "He was terrific."

After Paul left we sat quietly together holding hands. Kevin had had cancer and I thought of how lucky we were. I found myself flooded with sympathy for Lois, all resentment gone.

"I'll make a pot of soup and bring it over," I told Kevin.

He nodded.

I prepared a pot of lentil soup and, for the first time, crossed the boundary between Lois' property and ours once I saw her car in the driveway. I knocked on her door. She opened it a crack and looked out at me.

"Lois, I'm so very, very sorry to hear about Bob. He was a wonderful man and we both enjoyed talking with him." I held out the pot. "I've made you some lentil soup. Paul said you wanted us to know that you were alone here and I just want you to know that you can ask us for any help you need and that you and Paul are always welcome for dinner."

She stood behind the door, her face, impassive as stone, surveying me with such a clear hostility I felt physically assaulted. She finally opened the door just enough to take the soup and pull it inside, then once again closed the door until it was only open a crack.

"Paul and I will do fine. We won't be coming to your

house for dinner or anything else," she said then slammed the door in my face.

I stood there stunned at her response and Lord help me for just one moment, but one I'll always be ashamed of, I thought, serves you right to lose your husband, you bitch. Then I thought of Paul, the friendly warmth of Bob's voice and his welcoming smile and knew that I needed to move; the isolation of this road was destroying the person I'd believed I'd grown into until that moment. I was shaken by this side of me that was so without charity. I tried to justify it by her cold rejection of my attempt at sympathy, but in the end my personal behavior could not be based on her; it had to be based on my internal code of what was right.

The next morning the emptied pot was on my doorstep with no note of thanks. Something shut tight inside me as I put it back in the cabinet. I knew that I would never again say a casual hello to Lois; her reluctantly returned hello could never provide any satisfaction. Kevin looked at the pot silently as I set it in the cabinet. "You did the right thing," he said. "No matter what she does."

"Yes. I'm not sorry I brought the soup, if only for Paul."

That evening we went to Bob's wake. We struggled to find a space in the parking lot and walked inside to a room humming with people.

I looked at Kevin in surprise, and also relief that we would not be among only a few.

"Bob was a salesman," Kevin said. "He knew a lot of people. Let's find Lois and Paul and pay our respects and then we can leave."

Paul hugged us and greeted us warmly, thanking us for

coming. "My mother is over there," he said pointing to a small group of people, nearly all men.

"Let's get this over with," I told Kevin as we walked toward the group.

We walked over and Lois turned as a man in front of her pointed to us. I was stunned yet again; Lois looked beautiful. She wore make-up and a flattering blue dress, silver earrings, the faint scent of expensive perfume drifting toward us. Her eyes shone, narrowed at the sight of me, then brightened as she looked at Kevin. He didn't miss her response and put his arm around me. We repeated all the things you say at this type of event, Kevin offering any type of assistance she might need.

She smiled warmly, staring directly at him as though I wasn't by his side.

"I'll be fine," she said. "Paul is going to transfer to a nearby community college."

He nodded, turned, and we made our way to the door.

"You know," I said thoughtfully. "I worked with a number of female clients who said they had no women friends, that they only trusted men; perhaps Lois is like that also."

I'd resolved, after my cruel thought, that the answer to my isolation was to move, to recreate the bustling streets and easily accessible activities of my childhood.

"I can't live here anymore. It's too isolated," I told Kevin a few days later.

"Summer will be here soon," he said.

"Yes. But then winter will arrive again."

It was a difficult discussion because I proposed moving

to Portland, a city where I had many connections, but which left Kevin farther away from work.

"A geographic cure isn't the answer," he said. "You have to tackle your internal loneliness."

"You travel all the time," I said. "You never have a chance to be lonely."

With the first spring thaw I determinedly set out to house-hunt and after six months found one that worked for us. It was near the university, a few houses down from the library, had a gallery, three restaurants, bakery, a convenience store within walking distance and was just one mile from the train that would take Kevin to work. I loved the neighborhood and after a week Kevin loved not driving to work, the extra half-hour of travel consumed by the work he did as the train chugged along.

One December afternoon Kevin and I removed the last of our belongings, did a final cleaning of the house before the new owners moved in, and walked around the land for a tearful good-bye to this property we loved. Lois, watching through her window, came out, strode with her usual briskness over the property line, and hugged Kevin, wishing him the best of luck in his new house, then, as if I wasn't there, went back into her house with a good-bye wave at him.

Why she disliked me, and her refusal to acknowledge my presence, didn't matter anymore and, as we got into our cars to leave this road behind forever, I wished her peace in whatever journey she was on.

Heat

The heat, that summer of 1957, was a dense web that wrapped itself around you like an infestation of leeches. It draped New York with the particular hazy dreaminess of an impressionist painting. I was thirteen and had my first job that summer, stapling tags onto winter clothes in the warehouse of a department store. Previous summers my brother and I roamed the streets, stole candy, and drenched ourselves in opened fire hydrants, reveling in the frigid spray like puppies. We darted into the rundown, air-conditioned movie theatre across the street, when the exit door opened and the paying patrons left. We sucked ice cubes till our lips were blue and trembling. My mother worked as a file clerk in Manhattan for fifty dollars a week after my father deserted, leaving us free to ramble as we chose, quickly spending our twenty-five-cent allowance. That summer, tired of doing without things my mother couldn't buy and I couldn't steal, I wanted an independent income.

As a minor, once I found a job, I needed working papers. One Thursday I hopped a train to lower Manhattan to be examined by a state physician who'd sign off that I was healthy enough to hire. The cavernous waiting room, steamy with a mob of sweaty, grumbling kids, had tall, dust-coated windows that clouded out the sun. Nervous energy blistered like electricity under the rumble of voices. The heat blurred everything in a slur of colors. A few ancient floor fans whirred half-heartedly but the only effective one rested on the desk of the receptionist who ushered us into the doctor's office, first-come, first-serve. Everyone fidgeted on the hard-wooden benches while the receptionist edged dangerously close to the fan and drank endless glasses of cafeteria iced tea. Her voice was high-pitched and whiny, transforming each name she called into a personal complaint. She glared at us through heavily made-up eyes as though we were responsible for the heat.

Some kids, anticipating the boredom of a long wait, had come with friends. The thick humidity flattened their shrieks and loud voices. Sometimes, horsing around, a kid was shoved off a bench, thudding to the floor with riotous laughter. "Stop that," the receptionist snapped, briefly relinquishing her stale fanned-breeze to point like a spaniel fingering prey. The noise would lower then rise again to its previous level.

The majority of us, here alone, focused on our shoes or read a book, our fingers depositing moist prints on the pages as endless moments passed. Damp yellow circles stained the underarms of boys' shirts and perspiration glistened on cheeks razor-nicked by those new to the art of shaving. The pancake make-up most girls wore was etched by trails of sweat. I crossed my arms to conceal bra and nipples outlined beneath my damp clinging blouse and tried to read.

The receptionist finally called my name, running the syllables together so I didn't recognize it at first. She repeated it sharply, and when I realized she meant me I stood. She scowled as though I'd been hiding, her teeth angrily chewing her lower lip, and pointed, "In there," then checked my name off the list.

The doctor's office was dank with humidity, every surface pearled with drops of moisture. Under the bright overhead light, an elderly, bored man with thin lips, and a stethoscope round his neck, sat on a stool. His glasses were flecked with dust or cigarette ash, his shirt collar darkened by perspiration. He barely glanced at me as he took my working papers, rested his cigarette in an overflowing ashtray and placed the stethoscope on my chest. "Cough," he said. I offered an exaggerated imitation of a bronchial cough from six months earlier. He nodded, performed a cursory examination of my throat and ears, felt the glands on my neck, then scribbled his signature on the papers and gestured me out with a wave. The cigarette was in his mouth before I closed the door behind me. It took maybe two minutes and I felt foolishly pleased as though I'd accomplished some great feat. The secretary threw me a dirty look when I passed her, then massacred the next name on the list.

Outside, I pulled on my sunglasses to avoid the blinding glare off office windows. Humidity descended like a shroud over me. People ambled listlessly along the streets, a particular, usual New York briskness submerged in some heat-induced trance. As I walked to the train station, a rare breeze off the water was contaminated by the heat and utterly without value.

My mother and I, in what would become a daily ritual, left together on my first day of work. She gave my seven-year-old brother a quarter and the information that she'd secured the upstairs neighbor's promise to keep an eye on him. He looked at me sorrowfully as though I was abandoning him but rather than guilt I experienced a surge of envy at his freedom. I felt I'd passed over some pinnacle into adulthood and could never be that wild again. My mother regarded him doubtfully despite his promise to remain on the block, keep his key around his neck and not get into trouble. She was self-educated, having completed only fifth grade before forced to go out to work, but especially savvy. She'd acquired an immense vocabulary reading that she employed each Sunday to complete the New York Times crossword puzzle. She warned him, "Don't underestimate the dangers of the street, no matter how smart you think you are. Stay close to home and don't go near the boys on the corner." She kissed him good-by, tucked Crime and Punishment into her purse, and beckoned me out ahead of her after tossing a final "Remember what I told you," at him.

A few neighbors yelled "Good luck" when we passed. I flushed with pride, even knowing that my accomplishment was merely a natural consequence of growing older. My mother waved back, also proud. The brisk clicking of her high heels was drowned by the rumble of trucks and irritated car horns. She expertly navigated the cracked sidewalks, never once catching a heel. After a block my dress and crinolines were sweat-soaked and heavy, while her shirtwaist remained crisp, short auburn hair unruffled. Although only seven in the morning it was hot as noon. A few people were still pulling in their mattresses from the fire escape where they'd slept to escape the deadening heat.

"You think I can trust him?" she asked, referring to my brother. It was a rhetorical question but, knowing she couldn't, I answered, "Sure." Then to take her mind off him added, "It's hot as hell."

She smiled at my nonchalant use of the word hell and answered. "Summer is always a scorcher in New York." Halfway down the next block was the Italian deli, the familiar, summer-rancid smell of the streets layered beneath garlic, oregano and tomatoes like perspiration under heavy perfume. She stopped and smiled conspiratorially at me. "In here, just for us today." Five minutes later we emerged with scrambled egg and hot pepper sandwiches in two brown paper bags rapidly darkening with grease, a treat to honor my induction into the labor force and the reason we hadn't packed sandwiches.

"Thanks, Ma," I told her and she nodded. A block further was the new movie theatre, holding out the promise of sleekly clean floors and well-cushioned seats. A man in jeans and white undershirt balanced on a ladder to change the marquee. I stared at the eight letters he'd clicked into the white rows and tried to guess what film would play that afternoon. I fantasized going home, under pretense of a stomachache, and later sneaking in through the back door with my brother when the first matinee let out, more of a challenge than our nearby theatre where the ushers had grown lax on minimum wage. My mother looked at me sternly as though she knew what I was thinking and I quickly faced forward. She examined her watch and speeded up. We marched silently to the train station.

As we waited on the platform, I looked at my wrinkled dress and asked, "Do I look OK?" She tossed a venomous look at a man who'd shoved her and casually mashed her high heel on the toe of his polished shoe. He stomped away, mumbling under his breath. She examined me then assured, "You look very nice, very business-like." The train roared to a clanging stop in front of us, and everyone pushed into a car so mobbed we didn't even sway once the train started rolling. Overhead fans served only to disperse the acrid scent of perspiration throughout the subway car. Sweat dripped down my back and under my armpits and I was sure I'd absorb the stink of the subway car and be embarrassed my first day at work. My mother left her book in her purse and talked about the most obvious topic.

"I don't remember heat like this," she said solemnly. "Even here." Many of those crammed against us nodded and one man added, "Amen." She smiled at him and said, "See, everyone agrees."

"I agree too, Ma," I told her.

My stop came first and she nudged me toward the door. "Have a good day. Work hard." With only two stops to go, she pulled out her book as the door closed behind me.

New York was always being torn down or built up, a shifting landscape of old homes replaced with office buildings. A block from my job the pounding of heavy equipment at a construction site made my ears ring. The construction workers were covered with the fine, white dust of destruction. I passed, eyes down, afraid of catcalls although, at five feet and ninety pounds, I'd never inspired lust. Still, I imagined that they might practice on every female who walked by. I circled rubble and broken glass and swung my lunch bag as though holding my mother's hand, although I hadn't for years.

The office building had three floors, the lowest one the warehouse. The secretary announced my name over the loudspeaker while the fan blew her hair gracefully around her face like a television commercial inspiring my usual resentment at my tight curls. A moment later an attractive, middle-aged black woman with conked hair, brown-rimmed glasses, and mauve lipstick opened a door and beckoned to me. She wore jeans and a blouse and her eyes flooded with amusement at my dress as she held out a callused hand to shake. "I'm Alice. Come upstairs and meet the boss then we'll go to The Floor."

I followed her to a small, air-conditioned office. The man behind the desk stood when we entered in and came around it to greet us. He was shaped like a banana with a strange forward slant to his posture. He studied the working papers in his hand, then looked up and through me as though I was transparent. He was already turning away as he said, "Well Michelle, work hard, listen to Alice, don't get in trouble and it'll work out." I nodded and he returned to his desk, shuffling papers, his manner indicating I was already forgotten. His absent-minded dismissal of me, relegating me into the anonymous pool of another poor kid working in a warehouse somehow electrified me. I knew at that moment that, as an adult I would work for myself despite the legacy of poverty that weighted the odds against it. Only I would have the right to decide how hard I worked and its value.

The Floor was exactly that, running the length of the building and, since factories worked one season ahead, swirling with wintry wool clothing. A few tall floor fans were scattered around, but the corridor between each row of clothes was so narrow that a fanned breeze didn't stand a chance of penetrating. It was a giant walk-in closet crammed full, a good twenty degrees hotter than the offices, making it laborious to breath. Everyone was ruddy-faced and glistening with sweat. I was given a fat chrome machine on wheels to staple the price on each item. Coat and jacket sleeves rubbed my body like obscene gropers. By the next day, I was imitating my more experienced co-workers, all teen-agers it seemed, who perversely, spitefully, wiped necks and faces and arms on the clothing they labeled.

I was clumsy at first and more than once stapled my fingers, but Alice remained patient and worked with me until I got the hang of it. Before she walked off she said quietly, "A dress like that, crinolines, not the best thing to wear here." I nodded, having already figured that out. This wasn't business…it was something else entirely. The next day I wore jeans and a long-sleeved shirt to prevent my skin rubbing against wool in the unflagging heat. When the day was over the bathrooms filled with kids washing with paper towels and changing into shorts and tank tops.

All I remember of the work force, although there were girls my own age, is one woman beside Alice, and three boys. Mitch had the slicked back hair of a greaser, tight jeans, a half-open shirt, and a confident smile. He was a stereotype of one breed and David and Mark were stereotypes of another. They were crowned with the same kinky Jewish hair as mine, and wore brightly striped shirts and jeans that emphasized their stockiness. They lived near each other in the Bronx and came to work together. Halfway through the summer I went with Mitch to a movie, thrilled at having my first date with such a "looker," as everyone on The Floor called him. He necked passionlessly with me, as though it was a chore. I was too inexperienced and flattered to care. He left me at my door with a cool good-by kiss and after that ducked behind suits and coats when he saw me to avoid even a casual hello. The week before Labor Day he waved a list of girls that he'd made-out with. It comprised all of us on The Floor and included some of the secretaries from the second and third floor. Because I was a loner, I experienced a strange pride at being included, finally one of something.

David, Mark and I developed a summertime friendship, eating lunch, talking about the job, growing up, politics, and going to a hamburger joint and movie together with our first paychecks. One evening I had dinner at Mark's, a fussy, middle-class five room apartment with glass lamps, brocaded living room set and long, carefully arranged drapes in heavy red satin. There were a number of fans and I was as cool there as anywhere else that steamy summer with the exception of a movie theatre. Mark's mother dismissed me as a possible girlfriend for her son when she learned I lived in Williamsburg, a low-income ghetto. After dinner she didn't want the boys to accompany me home on the one-hour train ride. I remained firm despite her pursed mouth and shrill, "Why is it necessary, you're used to the neighborhood. The boys aren't." Mark was thrilled to commit this small act of rebellion against her. He and David complained about their mothers all the way to Brooklyn.

And the woman I remembered, the one besides Alice.

Her name was Mary.

Alice started me down the rows that first day, pushing the machine ahead of us, her deft fingers making fast work of sleeve after sleeve. We reached the end of the row and turned a corner. A woman wearing a drooping skirt and sloppy blouse turned at the sound of Alice's voice assuring me, "It's not hard. Just take your time at first." Her brown hair was wild. Her eyes, slanted in the manner that indicates Down syndrome, were thickly circled with black eyeliner, mascara smeared and beaded. Her mouth was blindingly scarlet, white teeth ruffled with lipstick. She was in her late twenties or early thirties with slouching shoulders and a full, fine body. She offered an enormous smile and a poorly articulated "Hello." I answered, "Hi," and smiled back.

"Get to work, Mary," Alice said, pushing the machine to the next row. As Mary turned away I said, "My name is Michelle. Pleased to meet you, Mary." She flashed another quick smile then with a glance at Alice began stapling with a practiced, smooth precision.

"She's harmless," Alice said when we were once again

buried in coats. "I know that," I answered, surprised. There were two Down syndrome kids on my block, a boy with cowlicks and a lazy eye and a fat girl who sat on the front steps greeting everyone who passed. They stayed out of range of the neighborhood boys who punched or teased them. Alice told me that Mary had worked there six years and I soon realized that after the usual "Good Mornings" she was treated as part of the warehouse scenery.

Things quickly settled into a boring routine, my mother and I traveling together in the morning, usually reading, shipments of clothes waiting each morning, smoking breaks, half-hour lunches, then home. At least once a day the boss checked up on The Floor. His rapid footsteps stopped at the beginning of each row then moved by so quickly I thought it impossible he actually saw how hard any of us worked. He always appeared before a break or lunch and his long body curving forward in its strange manner nudged me from my heat-induced, dreamy slowness. I would staple with the smooth, swift regularity of a clock ticking.

Each morning I exchanged hellos with Mary, touched by her quiet shyness, an exaggerated version, it seemed to me, of my own lack of confidence. Sometimes I shared a cookie with her at break before joining Mark and David to smoke outside, although usually she went off by herself or never even appeared. Her rows were done before anybody else's and I could often hear her say to herself, "Good work Mary," when a line was completed. She flashed her full-mouthed, odd smile to everyone who said "Hi," to her, however when the boss appeared she shrank, her head vanishing into whatever she was stapling, her back curving forward and her knees moving tightly together.

One particular afternoon, Mary was in the next row over, both of us buried in thick black coats with enormous brass buttons shaped like anchors. Their sleeves were heavy as five -pound weights and I was wiping my forehead and hands on the lining of one when I heard the boss growl, "What are you doing, Mary?" I jumped, wondering how I could have missed his arrival. I buttoned the coat and began to staple maniacally. A moment later, I heard "You're a bad girl, Mary. No break today"

I was astonished and stopped stapling. Mary a "bad girl?" She always worked steadily, lost in whatever thoughts she had until Alice tapped her on the shoulder to remind her of lunch or to go home. His footsteps thudded by. He paused a moment at the head of my row and I stood motionless, clearly in sight to see if he'd describe me as a bad girl also who couldn't have a break, but he went swiftly out the door to the stairs. I heard Mary's machine drag down to the end of the row and saw her shuffle like a frightened mouse to some suits against the farthest wall. "I'm sorry, Mary," I said, but she kept walking.

Alice called for break then and the click of machines halted like a field of crickets gone dead. I stood and stretched, eager to leave the building, but when I passed Alice leaning against the wall fingering her cigarette, I paused. She looked at me crossly, one eyebrow raised, and I almost walked past, but I thought of Mary without a respite from the deadening heat and stuttered, "The boss told Mary she couldn't go out on break." Alice remained silent. "Isn't that illegal?" I continued, embarrassed at the nervous break in my voice.

She stared at me impassively then said, "He's the boss." She straightened up and walked toward the door. "He knows what's legal. Keep your nose out of it."

I flushed red as she vanished. Mark appeared and grabbed my arm. "Come on. We only get twenty minutes, and one's already wasted." David came up behind me, put his hands on my back and shoved. "Hurry-up." I allowed myself to be gently pushed out into the street to smoke and pray for a merciful breeze.

The next morning, jammed between commuters, I asked my mother, "Isn't it illegal to not give somebody their coffee break?" She lowered her book and looked at me. "Did somebody tell you not to take your break?" She waited. "Not me, another worker," I said. My mother, usually champion of the underdog, astonished me by saying, "Let the other worker stick up for herself." At my puzzled look she answered, "It's part of growing up, learning how to take care of yourself. The world isn't going to do you any favors." She patted my shoulder and went back to her book. I didn't voice my thought, what if the other worker couldn't grow up?

After that incident, I grew aware of the boss telling Mary a couple of times a week that she was a "bad girl" who couldn't get her coffee break. I raged inside at the injustice, however, without Alice's support, I felt impotent and very young. I tried to approach Alice again, but she walked away before I could say a word. I got the message.

Briefly escaping the oppressive heat on The Floor seemed the only way to survive the job, but whenever I stepped out on break to smoke, the thought of Mary tainted my pleasure with guilt.

One afternoon I finished the last cigarette in my pack and wanted another. My spare pack was in my purse under my machine. "Have one of mine," Mark said and held up his menthols. "No," I answered. "I don't like that sissy peppermint flavor you smoke." He pretended to punch me and I ducked while David said, "No hitting girls." He narrowed his eyes and added, "Well, maybe this one." We were the only Jewish family on the block and growing up as a tomboy I tried to in vain to be befriended by the neighborhood boys who instead called me Kike and worse. This friendship, my first relationship of any sort with boys, was thrilling. I retorted, "I can take you both with one hand," almost silly with glee. "Go on and try," Mark retorted, in an unconvincing attempt at ferocity. "I will," I said, stepping up to him and curling a fist in mock challenge. "I'll be back in a minute to take care of you."

I swung open the door to The Floor and the dense heat inside closed around me like a trap. I was drenched within the few seconds it took to reach my row. I swooped down to retrieve my purse, then deliberately wiped the sleeve of a suit across my forehead. A soft whimpering from a row near the back wall stopped me. I was suddenly frightened, childishly imagining a warehouse ghost then chided myself and angled between heavy walls of wool to investigate, shielded from view by a long green coat with epaulets. Mary sat, legs sprawled, against the stained green wall. Her face was flushed, mottled with sweat and tears. Her eyes were screwed shut. She continued to whimper. The boss stood over her, narrow shoulders outlined by the wet shirt clinging to his back. He turned, zipping his fly, face expressionless. Sweat glistened on his upper lip and forehead. I began to shake and softly pulled in behind the coats until I was one row over from them. He strode past and I listened to his footsteps reach the door and start up the stairs. My head pounded and I thought I might faint. My mind raced in a thousand directions, skittering away from what I was certain had happened, perhaps was happening regularly. I ran to find Alice. She had to do something. This was far more than deprivation of a coffee-break. She had just come back on the floor, cigarette still in her hand, to call everyone in. I stood in front of her violently trembling, sweat dripping down my face and barely able to get the words out.

I finally whispered, "Mary, the boss, he's..."

She interrupted, ground out her cigarette on the floor, then looked directly at me. "You didn't see nothing." Her eyes were hard and unrelenting as she shook her head angrily. "What the hell are you doing here? You're supposed to be on break."

"The boss..." I hoarsely began again, certain she didn't understand.

"The boss nothing," she said. "Mind your own business, girl. And you think about what you're about to say because I know you're wrong before I even hear it." She shook her head once more, her mouth crimped and furious and walked off, her shoulder slamming mine when she passed. I sank against the wall, dizzy and nauseous. Had I misunderstood? Had I actually seen anything at all? A moment later, Alice shouted, "Break's over. We've got a whole new shipment to finish today. Come on people." She stood backlit in the doorway. Her hair, in response to the intense humidity, defied her straightening and frizzed out around her head like dandelion petals. She clapped her hands, then came back in and passed me without a word. I lowered my eyes ashamed, although not knowing what of.

"Where did you go?" David said, then looked at me in concern and asked, "Are you sick?"

I stared at his round, wet face and brown eyes magnified behind his glasses and thought of telling him but instead shook my head dumbly. "A little sick to my stomach from the heat. That's all." I went to the bathroom and stared at my white, frightened face in the mirror. My lips trembled and a tiny muscle twitched beneath my eye. I sponged my face and neck with paper towels, took a deep breath and went back to The Floor.

I had nightmares, flashes of Mary's face lipstick-stained and blotched, the boss's body growing, towering, engulfing hers. Each morning I woke up swearing I'd tell somebody, but who was there to tell? Who could actually help some retarded worker in a shit-waged job? I didn't know. I wished, then, that I'd stayed home with my brother, a street child running wild in the heat. The summer is almost over, I told myself.

August was so hot that my mother let us move our mattresses and alarm clocks out to the fire-escape after we'd promised to be careful with her sprawling potted garden, a self-contained landscape of beauty she sometimes barricaded herself in with a book. The snores of the man upstairs interrupted my sleep and I tossed uncomfortably reliving what I was certain I'd seen. Rows of bedding lined the side of the tenement as everyone vainly sought relief. I was silent now each day, as I walked beside my mother to the train station. She asked a few times if I was all right and I told her it was just the heat, that it was strangling me.

"Yeah," she said. "It's bad."

Each morning, as I punched my card, Alice turned away with a brusque nod. I greeted Mary effusively every day, asked how she was, then gave her my cookies or fruit from lunch. She always answered, "I'm fine, thank you," in her shy flat voice, offering her wide-mouthed smile. I wanted to believe I'd misunderstood, still I worked as far away from her as possible. I cringed the two afternoons I was close enough to hear the boss say she'd been a bad girl and couldn't go on break.

In desperation, I tried to speak with Alice again. Her brown eyes were blank, her mouth pulled tight, arms crossed over her chest. She curved into herself like a turtle bracing against an attack and snapped, "What business is it of yours, what you think you know? Mary needs this job. Where the hell else is she going to find work? It's the boss keeps her on The Floor. You want to get her fired? Just shut your mouth.

Forget it." I walked away from Alice confused, her words suggesting how amorphous right and wrong could be, and making me question the wisdom of my intentions. I had no idea what Mary's life was like outside of The Floor, if she had parents or friends or a social worker. Maybe Alice was right - after all, what did I know?

Alice deviated from her position only once. Mary had a bad cold; her face flushed enough to suggest a fever. She sneezed through tissue after tissue, plagued by great, wrenching coughs. Alice assigned her to a massive shipment of cotton turtlenecks that didn't shed and when the boss appeared, she called sharply, "Mary, come here and help me carry these boxes out. No break for you today." He spun and stared at her, but she met his eyes full on as Mary stepped forward. He watched them retreat down the hallway to the storeroom and his shoulders tightened, but he went back to his office. Alice came back puffing, in bad shape for that kind of physical labor, Mary coughing and sneezing, her nose red and swollen, yet I thought I glimpsed relief in her eyes.

The boss didn't come down the rest of the week.

I woke up every morning feeling like a wild animal was trapped inside me, pushing at my chest and struggling to break out. I thought I might be wrong to stay silent, but I rather hadn't, I'd told Alice, who else was there that could actually help? One morning sardined beside my mother on the train, I asked, "Ma, what can anybody do if they think they're doing something wrong."

She looked at me, putting her finger in the page of her book and asked, "You've done something wrong?" "No," I said hastily. "I just wondered. How do you make it right?" She lowered her book and leaned closer, her lips against my ear, so that I might hear her over the roaring of the train. "You're talking about Yom Kippur, what it's about. Atonement. That's when you ask to be forgiven. You often can't make right what you did wrong, but you try to do better, to be a mensch." The sentiment of her words, the irrevocability of wrong deeds, made me want to cry. She examined me with some concern, but wisely remained silent, waiting. I finally asked, "What if you don't think you can do better in a situation, if it seems impossible?" I thought of my father's desertion, my mother's low paying job, Mary's helplessness, and blurted out, "It's such a bad world. How can you do anything?" She shook her head. A flicker of anger mingled with sadness, filled her eyes. "It's impossible to change the world. You pick your battles. Figure out which ones you stand a chance of winning and then just let go of the rest or you'll make yourself crazy." She smiled sadly. "Such a tough lesson to learn, to figure out what you can actually do, sometimes even to figure out in the first place if you've done wrong or right, and sometimes you can't...you can only guess." She tsked sympathetically and continued. "In this world there are people with power and people without it. I think those without it can give only compassion freely, they don't have anything else in abundance." She put her hand on my shoulder and said, "If you atone on Yom Kipper, search your soul for answers, and try to make up for your mistakes, improve things in your little world, you've done the best you can do, and nobody can ask for anything more."

I was disappointed by her response, expecting some Yiddish-socialist doctrine that needed only a leader to be enacted, a movement like one that came years later - MLK and civil rights. But she'd offered the only way most of us can possibly succeed, by doing the best we are capable of.

I quit a week before Labor Day, the same day Mitch's list made its appearance. I gave Mary a tiny box of chocolates and hugged her good-by. She accepted it with her usual shy smile. Mark and David were surprised, but promised to keep in touch. They gave me a pack of cigarettes as a going away present. Alice shook my hand good-by and wished me luck. She stared thoughtfully for a few moments, shook her head, then came up close to me, her toilet water heavy in the summer heat, and asked, "What's the cheapest commodity in the world?" Surprised at her question, I thought for a few moments before shrugging and answering, "Tootsie Rolls." Something in her seemed to lighten at my answer and she threw her head back and laughed a little too wildly. When she stopped, her eyes were wet, and she rubbed her sleeve over them. "We are," she told me. "We are." My stomach tightened as she walked away. It was the last time I saw her.

My brother was glad to have me home. We filled the days with movies and fire hydrants, sneaking onto the subway a few times and going to Coney Island. I stole a record number of ice pops and frozen ice cream cones those last few weeks of summer. I stole other things, recklessly, wantonly, as if defying somebody to challenge me. Once I walked out of the department store whose warehouse I'd worked in carrying a pair of shoes in my hand. Nobody stopped me.

After a few desultory phone calls, Mark, David and I gave up.

I took a job in a hospital the following summer, filing endless folders in a dusty basement and then another job the following summer, and then another, each summer melting into each other in the heat that, to me, never quite approached 1957.

After I left The Floor, I forced myself to forget about Mary, but certain things resurrect that bright sloppy smile still, the opening line of "All Along The Watchtower", "There must be some way out of here, said the joker to the thief," the photographs of Diane Arbus and, a few years ago, the film, The Dream Life Of Angels. There are others that appear unexpectedly, evoking that last summer I thought of myself as a child.

. After high school graduation I held varied jobs, married and had two sons. I became part of the feminist movement and worked with abused women and children, then seventeen years later, after my divorce, hocked myself well over my head and went straight through school till I had an MSW. After my mother died, I moved to Maine. I had a few jobs in community health organizations working with both the poor and disabled, then as soon as possible started a private practice with a sliding scale.

One hot summer day a woman came into my office while I was doing paperwork, leading her Down syndrome daughter by the hand, a girl of nineteen who had been raped. They lived two blocks from my office, a manageable distance for her child to navigate. The mother had no insurance but could swing ten dollars a week. My office was air-conditioned and we sat comfortably, the girl staring at the floor while the mother spoke and I listened. The child answered the questions I asked her with a flat yes or no, never looking up at me. Her dark hair was neatly cared for, her worn jeans spotless. The mother held her hand the whole time we spoke. I took the case.

That Yom Kippur I walked the beach thinking about the world I alternately label beautiful and horrible, of the way atrocities seem to repeat and repeat and repeat, of the ambiguity of too many things. I watched the tide, tossed bread to the seagulls, thought about my mother and hoped I was doing the best I could.

On the Fire Escape

I recently read that New York City is installing fireproofed stairwells that will render fire escapes obsolete. I can't imagine New York without this icon of tenement life. Fire escapes were a city within a City. Life unfolded there: exploits of husbands, wives, delinquent children, anger, arguments, beatings, desertions. Vital information was disseminated, and they provided an escape hatch from boredom when unsuspecting parents slept.

The fire escape of my childhood was a peculiar sunroom allowing the pretence of gentility in our poverty. We camped there, sans tent, sleeping bag, and Coleman lantern. The summer air wasn't spicy with pine but with something stale, indefinable, blowing in from the East River. I'd stare at the sky through a corridor of water towers and television antennas. The clear, sharp beauty of the moon and stars was often dimmed by light pollution, but on certain nights the Milky Way asserted itself, a hazy tributary spilling over. I read propped up on pillows as the evening light slowly diminished, and I slept to a lullaby of backfiring cars, rumbling trucks, and kibbitzing of firemen from the firehouse across the alley.

The limitations of a three-room apartment extended the usefulness of our fire escape. It was a showcase for my mother's garden every spring. The deprived gardener in her was somewhat appeased as she dug her fingers into the potted earth. Gardening provided an affordable resource for her immense creativity. She was a woman forced into conformity by the circumstances of single-parenthood; this glorious sprawl was the antithesis of her harshly regulated life.

My mother married when I was four. I met my stepfather on the steps of city hall. He knelt to introduce himself. I knew even then that he was handsome, the dark flawless skin, straight nose, and slightly slanted eyes that drew women's attention.

He smiled, pulled a card from behind my ear—the Queen of Hearts. "A heart-breaker," he said. He closed my fingers around it.

I imagined him building a house of cards for us, walls brilliant with hearts and diamonds, spades and clubs, shimmering faces of kings and queens, jacks like sentries. I rested my head on his shoulder when he lifted me into his arms, and we went home to celebrate with cake on the fire escape, passing pieces to the neighbors.

My brother was born soon after. My stepfather pulled the Ace of Spades from behind his ear and shook his head. "How the hell did that happen?" He pulled another, the King of Diamonds, life of wealth. "Better," he muttered.

My parent's marriage was a bittersweet six years of repeated separation and reconciliation. In this neighborhood of arrivals and departures, I felt anguish but not surprise when he left. The years he lived with us bestowed temporary privilege; I was one of the chosen, the existence of a father granting protection from the boys who stalked fatherless victims.

He worked nights as a cab driver, and we shared the fire escape while my mother worked days. My brother laid on a blanket between us, first a scented bundle of talc, later a toddler who needed close monitoring, then a kindergartner with more sophisticated needs. My stepfather stretched over the old blanket, eyes closed, smoke curling from his cigarette, and listened to the ballgame. We heard about events we would never be a part of, a world as remote as the moon.

Our neighbors crowded onto their fire escapes weekend afternoons to listen to ballgames on our blaring radio. My stepfather aroused the tenement community to passion previously reserved for battles, slammed doors, gossip. They hissed when the other team scored a point, cheered wildly when the Dodgers made a home run, their victory our own by proxy.

"A good choice your mother made," the upstairs Lithuanian woman told me when we passed in the hall, as though my mother's shrieks of fury at my stepfather were beneath the range of human hearing, like a dog whistle.

My stepfather was a compulsive gambler who rarely won. He called Las Vegas the City of Churches and Schools, spoke of gambling casinos as holy sites, chorus girls as nuns robed in gauze and sequins, croupiers as novice priests. He drove his cab to raise stake money, rarely leaving enough for household expenses. He was fun. He taught me to play the odds, to take a chance. We bet on whether a prowling cat would knock over the trashcan lid, whether the clouds would explode into rain, whether the fire alarm would clang in the next half-hour.

My mother raged at him when a month's rent vanished in a throw of dice or a just-missed royal flush. He didn't utter a word. Cigarette smoke veiled his eyes and an ironic smile curved his lips. He was relaxed, choreographing a ballet of cards across his fingers. Driven to desperation by his smirking silence, she once chased him around the apartment with a high-heeled shoe, shrieking, "Answer me, God damn it! Answer me!" He remained silent, strangely jovial as he evaded her blows. After she left for work, he joined me on the fire escape. His eyes seemed feverish. He whispered, "Your mother gets very overwrought about nothing." He stared into my face, demanding my agreement, refusing to look away until I nodded.

I imagined them trapped in the same arguments, growing grayer and more infirm until one of them died. Then, when I was eleven, he was gone for good. His presence lingered in an envelope with twenty dollars slid under the door Friday nights and the occasional dinner my brother and I had with him. He was like a weary uncle, obligated to show up now and then.

Life continued.

My mother rose in the morning, hurried to the train after shouting good-byes over her shoulder. My brother went to school. I hopped a subway and prowled Manhattan, wide-eyed as a refugee. Before going home, I stole Twinkies from a grocery store. We ate them on the fire escape before my mother returned, burying evidential wrappers in the debris of a trash can.

In my step-father's absence, the apartment felt claustrophobic, as though one person less had paradoxically made it smaller. My mother vowed never to allow a man to insinuate himself into her life again. She was impenetrable, a fortress of conviction whose walls were never breached.

I needed the fire escape to breathe.

When I was twelve years old, I wrote my first short story on the fire escape—a piece of nonsense about the devil in a smoking jacket and an angel who reformed him. I fell into books, like Alice falling down the rabbit hole. Here I could melt reality into a dream and a dream into reality.

In December fire escapes blazed with Christmas decorations: gaudy red and white twinkling lights and thick ropes of pine that twined around the rusty bars. The dreary gray of winter was temporarily displaced by bursts of color. But our fire escape remained bare. As one of the few Jewish children in the neighborhood, I was the object of resentment and retribution from the bands of Catholic boys; I was mystified by their claim that I had killed their savior.

When snow fell in late January, the white-cloaked fire escapes seemed pristine. An elderly Russian neighbor inflamed my imagination by recounting stories of the Czar's palace brilliantly lit, candles shimmering through snowy windows, intricate ice sculptures a backdrop to skating, singing, feasts.

Then the snow grew filthy, melted, and left behind only a grimy ghetto. Hope seemed futile with this recycled evidence of our circumstances. Without the snow and flashy lights, it was obvious that fire escape ladders led only to the streets.

At thirteen, I migrated to my friend Lillian's fire escape, which overlooked the street rather than the alley. I felt liberated, as though this new view had somehow changed the circumstances of my life. We sat on her fire escape late one November night, striving for privacy. Buried in blankets, we spoke about boys, their swaggering confidence, their grease-sculptured hair, tight jeans, arrogant tongues. Our breath was white in the frigid air. Then, with the gift of intuition granted those intimate with violence, I felt a certain dangerous presence rise from the gutter. We fell silent. The local gang, in full war flank, appeared beneath us. We were grateful for our platform's height, grateful we had pulled the ladder up earlier. The shadowy figures claimed the streets. The Nazis, a group known to me as a Jewish child, seemed to assume a corporeal presence beneath us; they were men determined to destroy life. In later years, when I thought about that cold November air and that moment, I pictured the white cloaks and masks of the Ku Klux Klan.

I smoked my first cigarette on Lillian's fire escape, flaky contraband from her mother's purse. We alternately inhaled and coughed; it would be years before I'd smoke again. When spring appeared, Lillian, whose mother worked the nightshift at a factory, told me that her stepfather had begun to sexually abuse her when she was six. She whispered what he was doing, her fingers scraping the rust from the bars, her legs curled beneath her on the metal.

"I'll tell my mother," I whispered. "You'll come live with us."

She shook her head wildly. "No, no, nobody must know. He'll kill us. Promise me."

I promised. Lillian ran away from home the day after she told me, and I never saw her again. Desolate, I reclaimed my own fire escape.

My brother had not yet devised his own method of escape. I crawled out my window, book in hand, and sat silently beside him. He looked up at me, nodded, and then went back to his book. That summer we ate every meal out there and read side-by-side in a cave of plants. Everything seemed connected, sewn together: the alley, the firehouse, the tenements, the East River, the gutters, the rancid air. Concrete and asphalt stretched to the walls of the alley; we were in a box with no possibility of escape.

My brother was dreamier than I because he still had faith. My dreams were minor, grounded in the reality of a tenement dweller. I could imagine, but didn't hope. He remained good-natured with an intrinsic sense of morality while I easily stole from stores and lied. He was sensitive, puzzled by cruelty, slowly drowning in the abyss of the ghetto. I understood cruelty and strutted with a ferocity I didn't feel. We gradually lost each other as I grew tougher and his gentler soul was slowly submerged in the relentless bombardment of poverty.

When I was fifteen, the spring air seemed permeated with a restless buzz that inspired me to go . . . go . . . go. I went to Coney Island, wandered the beach, drunk on the salt air, the blaze of lights, the games and freak shows. I frequented museums and prowled the upper West Side, scowling at doormen, women walking dogs, mothers pushing children in expensive strollers. Later, on the fire escape, my brother read while I filled page after page with angry scrawls.

One day I woke up with a fever and my mother gave me money to take the bus to our doctor's office. My brother and I sat on the fire escape and decided we would walk to the doctor's office and buy Italian ice with the bus money. We roamed abandoned tenements, ducked into a candy store where I stole chocolate bars, stopped at the library. He waited patiently in the doctor's office where I was told I had the flu and needed to go to bed. We walked home, bought Italian ice, arrived just before my mother did.

Soon after that, my brother moved in with his father and almost disappeared from my life.

When I was seventeen, I gravitated to Greenwich Village—the sprawled expanse of Washington Square, the little coffee shops, and art house theatres. I wore black, ironed my curly hair, smoked, read John Barth, went to plays at the Judson Memorial church, prowled art shows. I saw the Weavers, heard the songs of Woody Guthrie, learned that there was a struggle for social justice. I was an immigrant in the Promised Land, newly arrived on the shore of activist ideals. At night I crept out to my fire escape and thought about what I'd heard.

I graduated in June. The guidance counselors had placed all the girls in commercial courses, never suggesting college. We were expected to marry as quickly as possible, raise children who would rent the tenement apartments when the dead vacated them. Landlords must be paid. Our children were expected to sit on those same fire escapes and repeat our lives. Evolution passed us by. The arty quaintness of our soiled brick buildings had not yet been discovered as desirable real estate, and we were the "ghetto dwellers." I got a job that barely paid enough to give my mother rent money and went on dates, pursuing what I'd been told was my only possible future. My time in Greenwich Village seemed a brief respite from the hard work of survival.

I met my first husband on a friend's fire escape, kissed him on my own, planned our wedding there, married, and moved to a basement apartment with dark rooms and half-windows. I got a job as a teletypist. My husband, part of an aristocratic family from Cuba, went to college, having never been informed of the destiny of tenement residents.

I wandered the streets in the evening while my husband studied. It was a neighborhood of poorly-constructed homes with claustrophobic front yards. Bulbs in the starved topsoil required replacement immediately after flowering. In winter the snow seemed permanently gray, falling from the sky without even the pretense of white. Everything was earthbound, too heavy to rise.

When I visited my mother, I crawled out onto the fire escape, breathed in the damaged air, and felt balanced again.

I worked until a week before the birth of my son. My husband, who had recently graduated and had a low-paying job, urged me to return to work as soon as possible, but I insisted on staying at home with my son for six months. There I swaddled him in blankets as the winter advanced and pushed him in his stroller regardless of weather.

My brother joined the marines. It was 1968. Fury and

disillusionment oozed from the country like blood from a wound. My brother was killed in Nam. A marine called me from my mother's apartment. Her screams, behind his voice, were the visceral, wordless shrieks of the mortally wounded. When I arrived, the two young marines looked away from me and quickly fled. I contacted my stepfather then crawled out onto the fire escape. I grabbed the bars and shook—each gasp of breath was a shout of fury at this limited landscape of sadness and defeat.

That day was the last time I was on a fire escape. My mother moved to Florida to begin a new life but returned to a tiny apartment in New Jersey. My husband and I moved to a little ranch house on Long Island, where my second son was born. Soon a tidal wave of frustration that could no longer be restrained, the women's movement, flooded Long Island. I was caught up in the undertow and amazingly, rapturously, I accomplished the impossible: I spit in the figurative eye of every guidance counselor I had known and began college.

I live in Maine now on a hilly expanse of boulders and evergreen trees. It has been decades since I've occupied that peculiar New York terrain perched between alley and sky, but it imprinted upon me certain proclivities: I require time outdoors on even the most frigid day. I view an extended segment of the outdoors as a room. The landscape around me undergoes a subtle reinterpretation—the trees stipple light like metal bars, and ice heaves in the road assume the aspect of cracked asphalt. The back door opens onto the deck with an intimation of my bedroom window opening onto my fire escape. My brother played the odds and lost; I played the odds and won. Yet I must continually remind myself that I am no longer dependent on the solace of the fire escape. The semicircle of forest around me opens onto multiple landscapes, all attainable by merely starting my car.

First Husband

Sometimes you jokingly refer to them as "your husbands," maintaining a certain ambiguity about how many there are (only two). It can be funny with the right people, a sort of joie de vivre in your telling which masks how difficult it all was. You met the first husband at a little social club organized by four close friends, one of them a high school schoolmate that you played handball with instead of going to classes.

"It's a secret location," he told you, "Just the building on the corner, dark shades, no street number. We don't advertise it because we don't want the gangs to break in; we've got beer and coke there. You should come."

Even though the room was dark and smoky you noticed him right away, dancing with a smooth practiced rhythm, his white shirt a shadowed flag in the dim light. When he turned and saw you also, something happened behind his eyes that you liked. He asked you to dance and you enjoyed the feeling of being effortlessly led, not knowing that he would always demand to lead. But back then, it was a relief and for some reason, during that first dance, you thought, I've been rescued, but didn't say it. He said it though, when the two of you were leaving each other.

"I thought you'd rescued me." he said.

You look at him with raw red eyes. "You never told me that."

But then, he rarely told you anything. He spoke about his life like reporting the daily news, impersonal with a minimum of detail: the death of his mother soon after his arrival from Cuba, his father's abandonment, his cousin who committed suicide. He cloaked himself in silence till it became the most notable thing about him.

You were both so young back then, just starting out in adult life really. You talked about all the things you'd do as though they'd already happened. You remember that time now as a series of events; days like tarot cards slapped onto the surface of your lives together: The wedding a snowstorm of blinding white and wet shoes, frost-bitten faces, biggest of the 1960's; a honeymoon of lost luggage, stolen wallets, misrepresented hotels, lost plane tickets; a bus journey home of exhaust fumes, greasy burgers, sore throats, burning eyes. You laughed when you were finally in that little basement apartment with its hollowed-out couch and window view of feet, cigarette butts, candy wrappers, swirling in the wind of passing cars. You told each other how being together made it all right, forgetting it happened because you were together.

There were days dragging yourself to work on a subway so crowded you thought you'd never get through the door. Those same days he went to college, eyes bleary from books of numbers and formulas and theories. There were evenings of cheese sandwiches sitting on the grass outside the airport watching planes fly in and out and he told you how they were designed, how he would design them, how he dreamed of airplanes; it was the most open he ever was, as though you weren't really there and he was telling himself a story. Then the serious black robes, and important parchment, and too-sweet cake of graduation and the resumes and calls and visits and a job and finally enough money, little though it was, and talk about starting a family.

You would do a family right, the memories of hunger and abandonment and violence making you both cautious - the two of you starting from zero as though nobody had ever had a baby before. You wanted the babies to be a part of the city the way you were, grounded in streets slipping into shadows and sun, museums flooded with color, the spice scent of a hundred cultures engulfing it. He wanted the house-grass-cozy America he believed he'd been promised.

Your neighborhood was bad but you were used to it, you weren't afraid until one night, six months pregnant and walking home from the subway, a local dope dealer slammed you against a wall, coming at you from behind like a predatory animal, panting hard and you got away and made it into a nearby bar. The bartender handed you the phone, told you to sit down and you did, blues music you could barely hear drifting around you in a swirl of boozy cigarette smoke while everyone ignored you. Your first husband showed up ten minutes later with a Cuban machete under his coat, one he could never have gotten through the airlines after 9/11. He wanted to look for "the fucker" but you just wanted to go home. Nobody bothered you again, like he'd drawn some kind of invisible cloak around you that shielded you from everything bad.

Once the babies came, with their tiny feet, small curled fingers, soft delicate heads, he reminded you of the drug dealer, the drunken fights outside the window, the darkness that filtered up from the streets. You were so wild with love then that you followed him into exile, to a small house in a barely-there town, on an empty road, while he left your two sons and you early morning and came home late night. You waited by the dark windows for his car lights, longed to hear an adult voice, and felt yourself falling into a pit, clawing at the edges to hang on so you could still see the faces of your children as they grew and changed and learned to say what they wanted.

You lay in bed some mornings, legs too heavy to move, Sesame Street echoing from the next room, and understood that you hadn't been rescued at all; it would take years to fully understand that only you could rescue yourself. You both were floundering, confused, with love a ghost so transparent it could fade with a single phrase, wearily reappearing at odd moments. Later, came the nights when he didn't get home until three in the morning and claimed he was working. Then the separate bedrooms, and the confusion, and the despair, and the tide pulling you along to this new place of total aloneness. You demanded a car, labeled it salvation; you fought, bitter desperation, anger, recriminations to his silent face, leaving you both taut with life's failures. You got one, dented and old, with one door that didn't work. It offered a roadmap to your life to come; consciousness raising groups, and a women's center you helped found and finally, blessedly, the college you never expected to attend. The years were a revolving door, the kids one year older, and stronger, and smarter, and more independent each time they came around and the two of you only visitors in each other's lives.

The end was shouted through veils of blame and petty vengeance. You were not kind to each other; you couldn't forgive each other for falling out of love. The divorce made you old. The children moved between you like precious objects neither of you could quite protect from harm. He remarried soon, and the three of you moved far away, your last act to save all of you from being drowned in fury.

You were together for seventeen years. Sometimes, at night, before you were too angry with each other to even share a bed, you talked: your friends, your family, things that were right, things that were wrong. You reminisced, even that young, about the past that you shared. You miss that now that there is nobody to remember when your brother got drunk just before he left for Vietnam and his death and waiting three weeks for his body. Nobody else remembers the name of the wonderful Cuban restaurant in New Jersey, or the espresso pot his aunt gave you not realizing you hated espresso, but happy to give you something she thought so American. He remembered with you when your mother died in a dumpy hospital in Jersey City; when his aunt of the espresso pot died and you cried more than he did, because you weren't afraid of tears, and the surgeon who attended your youngest son's tumor, a near dwarf with magic hands.

What you are most afraid of, however, is that you may not remember what really happened because he is not there to remember it with you, but then you often didn't remember things in the same way anyhow. You are sad that there is nobody, since his death, who understood what a crazy girl you were, with everything good and everything bad it implied. And also, now, you have a responsibility to remember that he loved folk music, not just Cuban songs, and liked going to concerts in Central Park and the Brooklyn Academy of music, and loved good Chinese Food, and how he'd mispronounced words, but could laugh about it, and the way you learned to share a thought with a single glance, but also the darkness in him that was stubborn, that held a grudge forever, that was still angry at you when he died, that something in him that maybe considered anger the most important remnant of the marriage beside the kids. What else, after all can replace the passion you once shared.

You've been married to your second husband for twenty-two years and still counting. This fit is easier, better, not rimmed with idealism, false hopes, talk of rescue. The two of you figure out how to make it work, day by day. The love is softer, more relaxed, more companionable. You met him on a street corner, when he was playing music like somebody lost, the piercing notes of the harmonica a sort of radar to help him find his way. You were tired by then of men, of their complex uncertainty about intimacy, tired of their difficulties with relationships, tired of trying to hear beneath the words and figure out what was being said. During the twelve years between these two men you were a patchwork quilt, pieces shredding off, new pieces sewn on, till it was no longer the you of the first husband. You'd read somewhere that every seven years all the cells in the body are replaced and you'd been replaced nearly two times over and imagined you were wiser. You weren't; you were only different, but maybe that's true for everyone.

You were truly devastated when the first husband died. Your anger had faded by then and you'd felt grateful he was somewhere in the world, that he too held the talisman of that life together you dragged behind you from long ago, resurrected at weddings, funerals, the birth of grandchildren. You were shocked at the knowledge that you would never see him again. But then, one day - he reappeared in your oldest son walking away, the shoulders slightly hunched, the familiar way of moving; your younger son's "Humph" when he wasn't quite sure of his answers; the curve of your oldest granddaughter's cheek when she turned a certain way. It stirred in you that old love in a way that was beyond time and anger, that came with the relief of how important it had been, none of it wasted. You thought of how it had all somehow come full-circle, that you were rescued after all.

The Season of My Grandfather

I was not eleven when I learned of my mother's father. At that time, my mother, my stepfather who I regarded as my father, my five-year-old brother and I lived in a sunny, three-room apartment in Brooklyn. My mother had substituted curtains for doors, missing on each room, thus permitting voices to drift through the narrow apartment.

I read as much as possible at that age, cultivating a trance -state that allowed everything else to float on the edges of my awareness. The walls of our foyer, lined floor to ceiling with my mother's books, offered immediate access to popular and literary novels, short stories and non-fiction. That Saturday, reading in the bedroom while my brother played on my parent's bed, I was vaguely aware of the intermittent rise of my mother's voice and my father shushing her. After ten or fifteen minutes my mother called me into the kitchen. I marked my page with a bookmark, rested my book on the bed then pushed open the curtain.

My parents were seated at the kitchen table, my father drinking a cup of coffee and dunking a buttered roll, my mother beside him, her mouth tightened in irritation. She pointed to a chair and I sat down opposite them at the table. A swath of sunlight fell across my mother, illuminating a nearly feverish anger in her eyes. Her voice was low and gravelly; a mannerism she'd cultivated to indicate barely controlled fury. "Your grandfather, who I don't speak to, lives on the Lower East Side right over the bridge," she bluntly informed me. "Your father, without consulting me, loaned him money last year." She turned to glare at him and he met her gaze without flinching, dipping his roll into the coffee and calmly eating. This contrast between my mother's volatility and my father's seeming serenity was a common one. Many years later I recognized the subtle ways he provoked her anger, presenting himself as the more reasonable of the two, a subterfuge that granted him a certain amount of sympathy.

My mother turned to me. "Every Sunday you'll take the bus to his tailor shop on Allen Street and pick up money until he pays back every cent."

The presence of an unknown grandfather was a surprise, but not a shock. My mother habitually shunned individuals for behaviors she interpreted as offences and people regularly shifted in and out of our lives. One was a sister she'd ignored for the span of my life who lived a mere six blocks away. Goldie owned a candy stand that remained open from morning to night regardless of weather. She opened on the most frigid of days, clad in heavy coat, gloves and kerchief. When it rained, she flattened herself against the building, a woman braced against brick, framed in gaudy bags of candy, gum and cigarettes. I'd discovered her identity through a friend who lived in her tenement.

The stand lay en-route to the grocery store and each week, in an exaggerated manner that guaranteed we'd be noticed, my mother would cross the street before reaching it, saunter along, then cross back once it was behind us. The only time I questioned her, she snapped, "It's my business, not yours." It didn't occur to me, as a child, that her business and mine intersected.

Secrecy pervaded every aspect of our lives, as familiar as breathing, so integrated into our day-to-day existence, I regarded it as normal. It remained the norm up to the day my mother died. She never revealed why she and her sister were enemies, why she refused to speak to her father, who my biological father was. Actually, she revealed so little about herself that for all intents and purposes her life began with my first memories of her.

But on this day: "Don't talk to your grandfather," she warned, staring at me across the kitchen table. "You have nothing to say to each other. Just collect the money and leave."

"Say hello," my father interrupted. He stood up, coffee cup and plate in hand. "Tell him who you are. Say hello for me." He ignored my mother's glare and brought his dishes to the sink to wash.

"So I should say hello?" I questioned my mother.

"Say hello since your father insists," she answered wearily. "Nothing else."

I nodded and looked over at my father who winked at me. My mother spun to glare at him, but he'd already turned back to the dishes.

Sunday morning my mother handed me ten cents for the bus and a nickel for a treat. "Remember what I said," she told me. "Get the money and come home."

I assured her I would, pulled on my sweater, and left.

The bus station on Sunday was always a maze of buses and people. I'd taken the bus alone over the Williamsburg Bridge by the time I was eight. In a neighborhood of single mothers and families where both parents worked while barely eking out a living, children were expected to fill their days after school. The presumption was that they'd do homework, chores, stay out of trouble. In actuality, tribes of unsupervised kids wandered the streets, keys on long chains flapping against their chests, indeed getting into trouble, though more often mischief. I was a loner who had difficulty making friends and when I skipped school I read, snuck into the movies, hopped the subway and explored museums, expensive department stores, innocently returning at school's end to retrieve my brother from the babysitter, a woman whose small apartment was jammed with the children of working mothers.

The bus driver watched me closely as I boarded the bus to confirm that I paid the fare. I dropped to a seat, wondering if his was a bus I'd previously snuck onto, a maneuver that required careful attention and was only possible during rush hour. As new passengers entered the front door, I would push through the crowds exiting the back one and lose myself in the mass of people, standing between the tallest ones I could find to avoid being discovered.

The bus was filled. A middle-aged woman smartly dressed in suit and gloves sat beside me, the last available

STEALING: Life in America

seat, after a Hasidic man chose to stand rather than take a seat beside a female. She opened the Mirror, a by-now long defunct New York paper, and began to read. I surreptitiously examined her soft pink lipstick and French twist, a popular hairdo the 1950's, thinking her appearance banal. While I considered my mother beautiful, her short boyish haircut, lack of make-up, and simple shirtwaist dresses lacked the offbeat drama that I imagined for myself one day. The bus circled the depot and drove past Washington Park where I'd learned to ride a bike, the renowned Peter Luger's restaurant, and a row of tenement houses with children playing stickball in front. It was a bright spring day with very little wind. The murky East River, which we walked across every Yom Kippur, reflected blinding slashes of sunlight that suggested a river of diamonds rather than one of growing pollution. Cars filled the bridge and we moved slowly. I stared into the windows of a passing train. A "greaser," with slicked back hair, dressed in black, caught my eye and winked. He was past in an instant, but I blushed, self-conscious about my growing interest in boys.

I leaned back in my seat and allowed myself to wonder about my grandfather. Would my mother look like him? Would I? Had he ever been curious about my brother and me? Did he know why my mother and her sister didn't speak? Would he be angry that I'd come to collect money? Why did he borrow it? How had he made contact with my father? The uncertainty of meeting him was suddenly frightening and I concentrated instead on the science fiction book I'd just finished, *The Dreaming Jewels* by Theodore

Sturgeon. There was much in it I identified with: I had no idea who my biological father was, I was often the butt of classmate's cruelty, I felt alienated from the world around me. Science fiction was my genre of choice. By the next year or so, I would recognize how much of science fiction at the time provided allegories of contemporary social problems, but just then it offered merely a glorious escape.

The doors opened onto a mobbed Delancey Street and I exited into a surge of people, an undersized, curly-haired girl in dungarees, brightly patterned sweater my mother had knit, and scuffed saddle shoes worn at the heels. Sundays, the Lower East Side bustled: the Orchard Street bargain pushcarts and stores, Essex Street indoor market with delicacies like Greek olives and herring salad, the kosher restaurants Ratner's and Katz, filled after the Saturday Sabbath when most Jews didn't travel. The vibrancy was intoxicating and I was caught up in the excitement of New Yorkers enjoying a day out. I looked through the window of Ratner's, envying the well-dressed customers patiently waiting on a long line for a table. I postponed the inevitable, strolling through the jostling crowds bargain hunting on Orchard Street. I touched everything, hats, jackets, scarves, ignoring the "Don't touch" from the sellers who knew I wasn't a customer.

Finally, I turned onto Allen Street, searched the house numbers and found the storefront my father had directed me to. The stairs were cracked, the iron banister rusty, the garbage pails overflowing. A large glass window fronting the lower floor of the building was filthy, the shadowy figure of a stranger behind it. My stomach tightened and I thought of going home, telling my mother he hadn't been there, but my lie would inevitably be discovered. Lying was a frequent defense and I couldn't risk the veracity of what I said questioned in the future.

I took a deep breath, slowly climbed the stairs, pulled open the heavy door and walked into a room cloistered against the outside world by bolts of fabric leaning against walls, on tables, piled one atop another, columns of wool, cotton, silk, that narrowed the room to a width little bigger than a cell. The breeze from the door as I entered had incited a swirl of bright lint into the air that slowly descended like embers. A massive pair of scissors rested on a large table with thick measured lines used to cut patterns. A man sat at a sewing machine pulled up close to the window to capture whatever light might stream in. He'd turned at the sound of the door and now sat quietly looking at me. I fell mute, wanting to flee, my mother's instructions to say nothing rendered unnecessary in light of my own shy silence with this stranger.

As if sensing my impulse to turn and run, he stood and beckoned me forward. I took a few steps in and examined him, a slender man in his late seventies, long wisps of gray hair electrically charged around a mostly bald head, glasses flecked with dust. Something in the Slavic cheekbones and set of the eyes hinted at our relationship. My mother's skillful sewing granted me an appreciation of beautifully made clothing and his heavy white cotton shirt and wool trousers, held up with suspenders, were impeccably tailored.

"So," he said in Yiddish. "You're Jenny's daughter and

you come for money, yes?" His voice was rusty, as though not often used.

Even as I nodded, I stored this new piece of information: my mother used the name Jean, now this stranger, her father, called her Jenny.

"Come here," he said in heavily accented English. "Nothing to be afraid." His lips curled and I realized he was smiling, a strange upward slant as though trying it out for the first time. I understood, at that moment, that he felt as awkward as I did and was determined to make the best of the situation. What is obvious to me as an adult, is his social ineptness, an indication of how tenuous his personal connections must have been. Here lay the roots of my mother's difficulty in maintaining friendships and the roots of my own inclination, long struggled against, to be disconnected as well. This, I knew even that young, was my inheritance.

I whispered, "My father says hello." He nodded, reached into his pocket, and without attempting to come closer, stretched out his arm and handed me an envelope. We were each uncertain of what to do next, then he shrugged his shoulders and turned back to his sewing machine. I saw, in this gesture, the precursor of my mother turning away from any situation that made her uncomfortable, my own disinclination to work at relation-ships.

A moment later he reached beneath the machine, pulled out a bottle of schnapps, took a long drink, and then stowed it beneath the machine again. He hesitated, but didn't face me again, starting the machine up instead. I turned and left, dust motes rising behind me like waving hands.

"So," my mother asked nonchalantly. "What did your grandfather say?"

"Nothing," I answered. "Didn't you tell me not to talk to him?"

I was mimicking my father, deliberately being provocative, angry at being chosen for this chore.

"Such a fresh mouth," my mother said and peered at me as if attempting to see in my eyes my visit with her father She turned toward my brother who read a picture book, his lips quietly moving. My father, a cab driver, was at work. After a moment she turned back to me. "So, your grandfather looked good?"

"I don't know," I answered. "I don't know how he's supposed to look. He looked OK to me."

"OK," she repeated as she considered my answer. She shook her head, then asked, "It's sunny, beautiful. Let's go take a walk, yes?"

"Yes," I said. Walks with my mother were always fun. She had an eye for unobtrusive details that transformed in new and exciting ways even our familiar neighborhood. She'd often find free art exhibits and would freely spend any extra money she had.

She turned to my brother. "Put the book away now. We're going outside." He looked up and nodded, hopeful that my mother would buy us an Italian ice. She hesitated a moment, then walked over to me, said, "Good job," and put her hand awkwardly on my head. I was flooded with warmth at her unusual gesture of affection and blurted out, "He took a bottle of schnapps from under his sewing machine."

She looked away from me, her eyes remembering something she would never share. "So," she said. "Still the bottle."

★

The following Sunday my grandfather had a large black and white cookie resting on top of a brown paper bag. He turned when I pushed open the door and stood. The lint swirled like confetti, then drifted down, some onto the cookie. "So," he said. "For you." He picked up the cookie, brushed the lint off the thick icing, and handed it to me. I was surprised, pleased that he'd thought about my visit, and certain that, before me, his customers and other shop owners were his only contact with the wider world.

"Thanks," I said shyly and took a big bite. The icing coated my teeth and I brushed my tongue over them, relishing the sweetness.

"So, Tea?" he asked.

I nodded and he put a small battered pot on a little hotplate, plugged it in, got a dish of sugar cubes and two stained glasses from somewhere, put a teabag in each, and stared intently at the pot, uncertain of what to say or do now that he had actually invited me to stay. I felt equally uncomfortable and concentrated on my cookie. Later we sat at a couple of ladder-back chairs, a silent duo drinking tea, a sugar cube between our teeth as we sipped the hot liquid. The quiet between us grew comfortable. I liked feeling myself one of two adults engaged in a social activity however lacking in conventional amenities.

"So," he said at last. "Your mother is well?"

"Yes," I answered.

He nodded and asked no further questions. When the tea was done, he stood, handed me the envelope, went to his machine and after a moment reached beneath it for the bottle. I said, "Good-by," and left.

Over the next two months, I took the bus in every Sunday morning. The Lower East Side was composed of Ashkenazi Jewish refugees from Eastern Europe and a smattering of Sephardic Jews, Hispanics, Italians that wandered over from Little Italy, and Chinese from nearby Chinatown. I loved the sheer diversity of this part of Manhattan; the melange of languages, the mix of foods with their various odors that roused my hunger no matter how recently I'd eaten, the colors of cheap fabric, high-heeled shoes, men's suits. I felt worldly there, as though anything was possible. The multitude of children walking the streets alone lent to my sense of independence; one of a citizenry distinct from adults, inhabiting a world they knew little about.

The weekly visits inspired a modicum of familiarity between my grandfather and me despite our joint inability to reach out. Each week he offered a black and white cookie or a bagel and a glass of tea. On a few occasions there was hard candy rather than sugar cubes and I assumed he'd run out of money. Each week he asked the same question about my mother and each week I answered that she was fine. My mother, after that first visit, didn't ask.

While my grandfather never once embraced me, his glance now seemed welcoming when I swung open the door to the rainbow swirl of dust motes. He never asked me about myself, or volunteered information about himself, perhaps believing all that was important was obvious: an old man with a thick accent who owned a tailor shop and was related to me. Conversely, perhaps all he needed to know about me was that I was his American granddaughter who crossed from one borough by herself as he had crossed Europe with his young family, and that I possessed the family sweet-tooth, slight statue, and its penchant for secrecy.

One morning, after our quiet ritual of cookies and tea was done, rather than immediately handing me an envelope with money and reaching for his bottle, my grandfather pointed to the back of his store, screened off with a curtain, and said, "Come."

I'd been curious about the curtain, but our time was very circumscribed: a sequenced series of activities and a ritualized ending. I followed him as he lifted it and walked through, finding myself in a room even more claustrophobic than the front one. An unmade bed in the corner with a sheet, old pillow and blanket, and cans of soup haphazardly stacked, indicated that this was his home. A tiny door against one wall suggested the likelihood of a bathroom. Cartons were piled one atop another, albums of 78's, some fur coats hanging on racks, a few black and white television sets, still a luxury in most households, radios, irons, toasters and other household appliances, toys, and endless boxes of books. I couldn't imagine what all of it was doing there. The floor was thickly overlaid with dust, but the objects were clean, suggesting recent acquisition.

"Pick, for you," my grandfather said. "Pick what you want. A present, yes?"

I had no hesitation; the books had attracted my attention immediately. I knew it impossible to do a thorough search, yet turning over a few books revealed one in a heavy leather protective case. I picked it up and turned to him and he nodded as I pulled it out and opened it. It was The Rubaiyat of Omar Khayyam, the Persian poet, complete with beautifully illustrated plates. I sank to the filthy floor and began to slowly turn the pages, enchanted by delicate exotic drawings and moved by the poems most of whose meanings I was too young to comprehend. The words flowed with a grace that pulled me along. I recited softly, to hear aloud the inherent music of the poem:

"Ah make the most we yet may spend,
before we too into the dust descend;
dust into dust and under dust to lie
sans wine, sans song, sans singer, and sans end."

This I knew was about death, about pursuing adventure while you could, about not being afraid to take a chance. I ran my hand over the thick, creamy paper embossed with calligraphic letters in heavy black and marveled at its weight and loveliness. I was enchanted by the illuminated gold letters, etched with tiny flowers, that began each verse. I understood then something new about books; they were not just a collection of words, stories, ideas, but also a home for all those things, and that the home could be as luxurious and splendid as the words themselves. After what might have been a minute, a half-hour, an hour, I looked up to see my grandfather watching me and nodding. His eyes were gentle; his face soft and relaxed. In the dim light I saw the handsome man he once was.

"Like your mother," he said quietly.

I realized how much he missed her, and felt certain that she must miss him.

"Why don't you and my mother talk to each other anymore?" I blurted out, then held my breath wondering if my question would anger him.

He stared at me, then shrugged and walked back through the curtain without answering. I stood up, clutching my book, and followed him out. He was already at his machine, the envelope of money on his big cutting table, and I took it and quietly left.

My brother played outside, my father at work when I arrived back home. My mother sat at the table drinking a cup of coffee, cigarette and crossword puzzle in front of her, pretending she wasn't waiting for me to come home.

"So," she said when she saw the book. "Lee the fence still using his back room, yes? He gets a cut, a few cents. That mamzer, bastard, cheats him good, not much money for taking such a big chance." She shrugged. "His business."

She took the book from my hand, pulled it from the case, and began to turn the pages. She ran her hand gently over the pages, entranced by the plates, suddenly oblivious to my presence. As she turned the pages, she recited a poem quietly to herself, then looked up, saw me watching her, closed the book and handed it back to me. "Very nice," she said.

"Can your father read?" I blurted out.

I saw the indecision of whether or not to answer even this simple question play over her face. She said. "A little Hebrew. My mother, dead now, nothing."

A sensation of light-headedness at having a question answered made me drop to the chair. She watched me with some amusement, then took a long drag of her cigarette and put it out.

I took a deep breath, deciding to risk it and asked, "Where did your parents come from? Where were you born?"

She smiled stiffly at me with her father's lips. "The old country."

"Why don't you speak to your father."

"Who knows?" She shrugged and went back to her crossword puzzle.

I woke up next morning thinking about my grandfather, feeling some strange measure of pleasure in having a family outside of my mother, brother and father, regardless of how disconnected we seemed from each other. There was something normal about knowing a grandparent as most of my schoolmates did, schoolmates who had aunts, uncles, cousins. I watched my mother dress for work in her neatly pressed shirtwaist dress and high heels. My brother and I ate our cereal quietly in order to avoid waking my father who'd just returned from his night shift on the cab.

"Be good, work hard," my mother told me.

She turned to my brother and warned him to be good as well for the baby-sitter.

"Don't forget to get your brother," she said as she left; words repeated every morning, although I'd never forgotten. My brother and I grinned at each other. I washed the breakfast dishes in the kitchen sink, reached for my brother's hand, and locked the apartment door behind us. After I dropped him off at the babysitter, I stood outside her building for a moment, struggling with indecision, then turned toward the supermarket and walked down the block that held my aunt's candy-stand. My stomach quivered as I approached it without crossing the street, stopping instead in front of it and browsing the candy. Traffic boomed behind me and the sun was strong enough to make me wish I'd left my jacket at home. I glanced up at Goldie, a stranger with my mother's face. She watched me with no expression. My heart pounded so loudly I was certain it was audible. I felt paralyzed; my eyes fixed on the candy, my hands, which I plunged into my pocket, trembling. Finally, she spoke. "So, if you have no money to buy, get outta here. I got no time for loafers."

I looked up to meet a replica of my own eyes, and stared into them. She stared back as though she didn't know who I was.

"So, you gonna buy something or not." The inflection of her voice was so much my mother's that for a moment I was disorientated. How could these women, so similar, be such enemies, or perhaps that was the very reason. Wordlessly, I pulled from my pocket the nickel I'd still had from the previous Sunday, gave it to her, and took a small chocolate bar. She took it and turned away from me, then kept her back deliberately turned. I waited a few moments to see if she'd say anything, make any sign of recognition, but she said nothing and I walked away on weakened legs, my stomach tied in knots.

Had I expected her to acknowledge me, to admit she'd been curious about me for a long time, to come around the candy-stand and put her hand on my shoulder or even, possibly, hug me, greet me like a prodigal child? Had I expected her to invite me in for tea and explain why she and my mother were enemies, ask if I had any ideas on how to mend the problem? Had I expected that she'd want to know me, what I liked, how I spent my time, who I was? I walked down the street with hot, flushed face, embarrassed at my naivete. How could I have expected anything more than what I got; she was my mother's sister and her father's daughter. It was not my first lesson about the differences between expectations and reality, not my first, but one that wounded me more deeply than I'd have imagined it could.

I never approached my aunt again. After we both left the neighborhood years later, I never learned what happened to her or her family.

"Last envelope. All paid," my grandfather said when I came in the door one Sunday. "No more visits." I was stunned, somehow unprepared for this. I realized then I'd imagined that my visits in this circumscribed space, with this tightly cloistered man would somehow continue, that over the summer he'd begun to treasure our relationship and his role as grandfather.

The seasons had transitioned from the coolness of spring into the sweltering heat of a New York summer, jackets replaced by sleeveless dresses, men's wool suits replaced by seersucker. It was this transition that had tricked me, the shift from one season to another imparting an air of permanence, impossible in the larger world, but especially impossible in this small one whose history was one of disengagement.

We sat over our last cup of tea. My grandfather had purchased apple strudel, a more expensive and festive pastry than a cookie. I glanced, as I had each week, at the curtain behind which riches lay. I received no further invitations and I wondered if Lee the fence knew every item back there and had taken my grandfather to task for a missing one. That said, I knew the sheer mass of objects made it impossible. More likely my grandfather, refugee from some European country that persecuted Jews, believed it possible and had bravely taken a chance. Perhaps he'd held his breath for weeks expecting to be punished.

In as casual a manner as possible, I broke our habitual silence and said, "I bought something from Goldie's candy stand. She didn't say hello to me. Do you see her?" I looked up knowing he saw the plea in my eyes for any information at all, anything to crack the cipher of my history. Indecision played across his face much as it had my mother's some months ago. I waited, but after a moment he only shrugged and took a bite of strudel.

I took a deep breath and tried another question. "Why don't Goldie and my mother speak to each other? What happened?"

He again remained silent and I knew that any secrets he had would die with him. There would be no revelations, no exploration of meaning, no attempt at reconciliations.

When we finished our tea, he stood, handed me the envelope, then sat in front of his machine. He reached beneath it for the schnapps, took a long drink, but didn't immediately begin sewing. I watched his hands on the table that housed the machine, a particular restlessness in his body culminating in one leg twitching, and a suggestion of defeat in the droop of his shoulders. I stubbornly stood behind him, holding the envelope in my hand. I stood there a full five minutes. He remained staring at the sewing machine and then, finally, began to sew. I turned angrily and stomped out the door, slamming it behind him.

"Here," I said to my mother when I got home. "Here, the last envelope." I went into my bedroom and waited for her to come in and speak to me about my anger, my grandfather, her past. She never did.

Years later, after my mother's death, a friend said that great secrets had been buried forever with my mother and it was a pity. I didn't feel that way. The day I'd slammed the door to my grandfather's shop behind me, something clicked into place, something almost like serenity. I understood that living my life would involve living with uncertainty, without answers, with secrets that would forever remain secrets, and that I needed to learn to be comfortable with it. I understood, also, to not judge the love of another by what I wanted, but by what they were capable of giving.

That autumn I turned twelve, my brother started school, and my mother threw my father out. She sunk into a sullen malaise, punishing my brother and me by frequently refusing to speak to us and often leaving the refrigerator empty. I spent time in the library rather than reading at home, my brother often accompanying me. It was there that I read Freud, marveled at the study of secrets, knew I would become a therapist when I grew up.

I saw my grandfather one more time. One day that autumn, I was prowling the Lower East Side, relentlessly handling vendor goods, defying them to chase me away. I'd stolen two apples, chased down the street by a fruit-seller who gave up; it was after all only two apples: but it afforded me a kind of triumph, a suggestion that any act I undertook in the future, no matter how dangerous, might be rewarded. I sometimes walked along Allen Street, briefly glancing up at my grandfather's shop before continuing on. This day, he was sitting on a bench, drinking a container of coffee and reading The Forward, a Jewish newspaper. Trees were assaulted by newly crisp winds that shook iridescent red and gold from their branches, a drift of leaves that blanketed the streets with a rich glory. I walked up to him, and saw that even in these brief three months he'd aged. He looked up at me as though I was a stranger, then went back to his coffee and paper. The season that had narrowly circumscribed our world had vanished in the autumn chill. I turned and left him behind, a solitary man, alone in a swirl of dead leaves.

Days and Days and Days
Between

It began with my husband's moaning as the soundtrack of a gray winter morning while oranges rolled across our kitchen floor like globes of sunshine. After what seemed like hours a shrieking siren announced the arrival of the ambulance I'd called. Two medics entered: one lean, with a gray pony tail, sad eyes of a witness, and cautious body language of experience, the other young, stocky, eager, already unfurling a stretcher. The older, wielding a stethoscope, knelt beside my husband and ruled out a heart attack, motioned his partner forward to ease Kevin onto the stretcher then they carried him out to the ambulance.

"Follow us in your own vehicle in case he has to stay overnight," the older EMT said.

I nodded and trailed them to the turnpike then braided my car through the chrome glint of speeding traffic. I felt myself at the edge of a frightening precipice; death, after all, is always the bystander waiting to step in. We parked and the two EMTs rushed Kevin down a corridor and into a cubicle, eased him onto a table and wished me good luck before they left. The cubicle had a sink and hand soap, medical implements, magazines in the wall-rack, and a perfectly centered watercolor of the ocean. A nurse threw a heated blanket over Kevin to still his shivering and assured us the doctor would be right in.

A few moments later a balding, seventy-ish doctor with a no-nonsense air of knowing exactly what he needed to do arrived, introduced himself and asked what happened as he applied a stethoscope to Kevin's chest.

I saw the fallen shopping bag, oranges rolling across the floor, Kevin's ashen face and clenched fingers, a memory replayed in slow-motion as if to preserve every second.

"He collapsed after coming home from the supermarket." Kevin, his eyes screwed shut, answered only, "Intense pain." The doctor offered an "I'm sorry" at Kevin's shriek when his probing fingers reached Kevin's abdomen.

"He needs painkillers," I demanded.

"First we need to find out what's wrong," the doctor explained. "I'll be right back." He vanished into the corridor, the starched white curtain rustling behind him. As the moments passed I repeatedly peered out into a corridor empty until Kevin's agonized scream drew the swiftly moving doctor and a colleague who dragged an ultrasound machine like a metallic beast on a leash.

"It's cold" one doc warned as he coated Kevin's stomach with gel and floated a disc over it. It reminded me of Monty Python at their most surreal: two docs muttering to each other as a large screen revealed my husband's internal terrain. Organs emerged and retreated like objects in a fog as we traveled the roads of superior and inferior vena cava and pulmonary veins, past fat spongy lungs, and stopped at the pancreas.

"This is it," the original doctor announced. His colleague nodded agreement.

"It's too inflamed to do anything right now. We need the resident surgeon to admit him."

"A surgeon?" I asked.

"It's easier in case he needs surgery."

He instructed a nurse to begin a saline and painkiller IV then left. She bustled around the tiny space. I finally went outside into the chilly sunlight to get out of her way and to leave as reassuring a message as possible on my sons' answering machines. They were very close to their stepfather and notifying them made the gravity of the situation official. Sirens from arriving and departing ambulances formed a howl of melancholy. I wrapped my arms around my body to still my sudden shivering, took a deep breath of cold fresh air and went back in.

Kevin's eyes were closed, his breathing shallow, the pallor of his skin signaling a body in deep distress.

"The surgeon will be here any minute," I whispered.

And then he was: a man in his forties with a fine haircut and intelligent eyes who exuded folksy, laid-back cheerfulness at odds with an aura of sophisticated, urban energy. He introduced himself, shook our hands, read the notes, explored Kevin's abdomen with sensitive fingers and offered a speculative diagnosis - idiopathic pancreatitis.

"Why did this happen?" Kevin asked hoarsely.

"Idiopathic means we don't know. We'll try to find out but in at least fifty percent of these cases we never do. The goal is get you better as soon as possible. Other than pain-killer there isn't any medication that helps. The pancreas just needs to rest."

He ordered a room, fished out a leather cardholder from his pocket, handed us each a card: the numbers of his cell phone, office, home, email address, and said, "It's easiest to reach me by email."

"The evolving nature of medicine," I joked, but my voice cracked removing any possible humor from my remark.

He smiled sympathetically, shook hands and left.

Kevin was wheeled into an elevator mercifully lacking Muzak, then to a room on the second floor and gently moved from his gurney onto a bed. A nurse switched IVs to a different pole, plugged in monitors, connected a self-administered morphine drip, while Kevin, with closed eyes, lay silently except for involuntary gasps of pain. I stepped into the corridor, my stomach churning, and encountered the unmistakable scent of a hospital - stinging, antiseptic, acrid; the unmistakable sounds of a hospital - that insidious hum from multiple machines in productive harmony, punctuated by frail voices being reassured; the unmistakable sights of a hospital - gurneys, racks of white bed linens, medical equipment. I peeked into other rooms and realized my fifty-five year old husband was the youngest patient on the floor. I took it as an omen that he wouldn't die here, as though death had a quota per age and hospital floor.

By seven o'clock that night I'd become familiar with the cafeteria, sitting room, wireless availability, coffee machines, and had spoken to both my sons, one in California, the other in Massachusetts about their stepfather. I promised to keep them informed as information came in. Kevin slept fitfully, jerking awake to administer painkiller then dropping off again. The surgeon appeared, checked Kevin's chart, nodded to me, quietly left. I would grow to feel he embodied something of the mystic in his arrivals and departures, intensified by the surrealist nature of hospital structure itself: life and death melting into each other and alternating shifts of strangers who provided stretches of intense intimacy before vanishing.

My legs, shoulders, back hurt. I stood stiffly, stretched, leaned over to kiss Kevin. "I'll see you tomorrow, but if you need me just call."

He nodded without opening his eyes.

I lingered at the door, looking at him, fearful that without my presence he would die, recognized it as a self-serving belief to counter my fear, and left.

I located my car in the unfamiliar parking lot, drove home through corridors of snow, beneath the stark night shadows of winter trees. In the kitchen I froze at the spot where Kevin had fallen. It was as though some indelible imprint remained that had absorbed the pain and fear from twelve hours earlier during a day that had seemed a lifetime long.

I tossed all night aware of the empty side of the bed. Absence writes its own book and this was only the preface; Kevin in the hospital, my fear, his pain, our uncertainty. This book would be both memoir and mystery. The possibility of losing Kevin, so integral to my life, was beyond imagining. I'd lived without a mate for the twelve years between marriages and had given up until I met Kevin playing the harmonica on a park bench one Saturday morning in Portsmouth, New Hampshire. Even seventeen years later I couldn't pass that bench without being infused with an almost supernatural feeling of destiny, that spot acquiring a vitality separate from location and appearance. A conversation about blues music had led to lunch and then dinner and then a courtship of a couple of years until we overcame the wariness left by our divorces. Like all marriages there were rough patches, but my husband was my partner in nearly everything; we relied on each other in ways so woven into our marriage we didn't even notice them anymore.

I gave up trying to sleep, prepared a pot of coffee, turned on my computer, read a description on the web that concluded: The heart, lungs, or kidneys may fail. If bleeding occurs in the pancreas, shock and sometimes death follows.

Not this time, I thought fiercely.

At seven I called Kevin.

His voice was weak and pain-filled.

"Did you sleep?" I asked.

"In a hospital?"

"I'll be there soon."

The snow piled along the turnpike and streets reflected a tarnished brightness in the morning sun. The parking lot of the hospital was immaculately plowed. I claimed a spot far from the entrance. It would be my spot, unlikely to be taken, and, after repetition, easily found in the dark.

Upstairs, the ward was filled with visitors tight-lipped with the strain of cheerful pretense. I caught my breath at the sight of Kevin hooked up to a heart monitor, its steady beeping a metronome counting life-minutes. It implied a frailty incongruent with our active lifestyle.

"Why the heart monitor?" I asked, dropping the latest New Yorker on his nightstand. "My heartbeat was too fast, so the surgeon hooked me up and started beta-blockers. I don't have pancreatic cancer, but still might be here about a month while they stabilize me and make some decisions." He hit the button for morphine.

Before I could frame a response, an elderly woman with dementia, housed in the next room, screamed, piercing howls of misery. I shut the door, reducing the screams to a faint echo. It felt ominous, an implication that our everyday world might eventually be locked away behind too many closed doors to reopen. I shook my head, fighting despair and said with an optimism I didn't feel, "A month is a long time, but then it's over." However, each sleepless night waves of fear suggested that this might be a rehearsal for permanence, a journey into the next stage of my life, widowhood. Each day when I arrived the hospital corridors seemed to resonate with regret that so much illness, pain and death were concentrated in this one particular place.

Kevin began to waste away, eyes often closed, lips dry and parched. He couldn't eat; the industrial table that slid over his bed held untouched Jell-O, apple juice, sherbet. He existed, like hummingbirds in summer, on glucose and whatever else was in his drip. It grew increasingly painful to witness what was happening but I forced a confident smile knowing I had become one of those tight-lipped people who'd mastered the art of false cheer. Kevin developed a love-hate relationship to morphine, loathing each slap of the button but counting the minutes until the next one. The surgeon turned up early in the morning, mid-day, evenings and offered encouragement telling us that it was a waiting game, Kevin's pancreas too inflamed to seek any further explanation or treatment.

"It's hard," he said. "Patience is hard."

He became my oracle; I depended on his assessment that we had a future. Each day was a repetition of the previous one. I worked on my laptop in Kevin's room revising an essay for a magazine while he slept and grew more alarmingly thin.

Five days into the hospitalization the surgeon told Kevin, "You're losing too much weight and since you can't eat, you need paranutrition. I'd like to insert a temporary PICC line tomorrow morning."

At Kevin's stricken look he added, "It's a very common procedure, it'll be fine."

He turned to me and repeated, "It'll be fine." He touched my shoulder and I nodded.

After the surgeon left, Kevin said, "I read about infections from the procedure." He shook his head. "Five feet of tube threaded to my heart, I'm not sure if I trust it." This was so unlike Kevin I caught my breath. I had always been the one to fret and worry, anticipating a problem months in advance while Kevin viewed worry as an unnecessary waste of time and energy.

I took his hand and said, "The surgeon knows what he's doing."

His growing weakness, near-emacing, steady reliance on morphine combined with this many projected days in the hospital in the age of managed care indicated the severity of his illness. My mind kept skittering away from the word death that sprung up in block letters whenever I looked at how wan and listless he'd become. Within a mere five days our lives had changed; so little time to make so much difference, to warn you about the future, to remind you that nothing is to be taken for granted.

When I arrived next morning, the surgeon had completed the procedure. Kevin's always slight body seemed even slighter, diminished by a construction of tubes, bags with various fluids, screens with flashing numbers like Broadway marquees. The idea that a tube as long as I was tall had been implanted in his body was shattering. Because of weight loss, his facial bones were sharply prominent, his eyes sunken, circled by a halo of darkness.

He pulled himself weakly to a semi-sitting position and showed me, on his laptop, an exchange of emails he'd had with the surgeon. Despite the hallucinogenic effects of morphine and pain, Kevin had researched articles on his condition and questioned the surgeon who responded promptly and with great optimism. I felt encouraged by this rallying of his usual method of investigating problems.

"It's not good despite the surgeon's optimism. People die from this."

I shook my head and said quietly, "Don't you dare."

That night I lay further engulfed by the possibility that this solitary darkness was my future. While we had the primary diagnosis of Idiopathic pancreatitis we had no idea of how long it would take him to heal, if this was a one-time -only attack and whether or not we'd find out the cause.

My frustration sometimes threatened to overwhelm me, but I recognized that the surgeon and hospital were doing everything they could.

By the end of the second week, Kevin's room had filled with flowers, plants, cards. Friends visited, phoned, sent silly gifts, including our friend Bill's ingenious structure of flour bags entitled "A bouquet of flours for you," which supplied humor for visitors. This hospital was geared toward families and our grandchildren visited frequently, enjoying the playroom with a dollhouse, games, cards, television set and snacks. My sons called him every day to offer support and encouragement and my California son and his wife flew out for a visit. The world we'd lived in attempted to reincarnate in the hospital, suggesting an air of permanence I refused to accept. The dripping of the IV, the beeping of the monitor, the sterility, I insisted this was only our present world. Kevin, the surgeon and I were a triangle, the surgeon the apex of our particular geometric design. Everyone else, no matter how faithful, no matter how dear, no matter how supportive, dwelled on the periphery of our lives.

One night, driving home beneath a slivered moon and sharp brilliant stars, I heard the Grateful Dead song, "Days Between:" "There were days and there were days, and there were days between." Since Kevin's hospitalization, time had altered, its dimensions shifted, days no longer discrete but rather one endless stream, day and night amorphous. We dwelt in a facsimile of Beckett's play Waiting for Godot, where the days lack differentiation as the two protagonists wait for Godot to arrive and give them a mysterious gift. We waited for the gift of recovery.

One morning when I arrived, Kevin, listless and skeletal, looked at me silently.

"What?" I asked with alarm as I gingerly maneuvered tubes to put my arms around him.

"They're afraid I'm developing pneumonia and now there's antibiotic in the IV. I'm losing weight every day. I'm in constant pain. I can't eat. I'm not going to get better." The despair on his face was both heart-breaking and resigned.

Kevin voiced the panic I'd been struggling against, waking in the night to think of the loneliness of widows, a particular condescending attitude I'd noticed toward older women who make their way alone in the world. My head began to throb.

"Sleep," I said, squeezing his hand. "I'll be right back."

I ran down the hall and into the little medical library, with its shelves of technical books and journals, and a telephone connected to the outside world and called the surgeon's office. "This is Michelle Cacho-Negrete. My husband, Kevin Smith, is getting worse. I need to speak with him."

"He's got surgeries back to back, but he'll call as soon as he can," she said comfortingly. "He's closely monitoring Kevin."

I hung up and for the first time quietly cried. Kevin was asleep when I got back. I settled into the chair beside him, opened my book and reread the same page ten times. Finally the surgeon appeared.

"Am I going to die?" Kevin asked, the surgeon's presence awakening him.

"You're healthy despite being so sick," the surgeon answered assuringly. "You'll get well."

He laid hands on Kevin's abdomen like some revivalist preacher and stood quietly like that for a few moments with closed eyes. I was reminded of having long ago seen, with my mother, Oral Roberts, a faith healer. He too had laid hands on a gravely ill man who appeared to recover. The surgeon opened his eyes and repeated with such confidence there was no doubting him, "You'll get well."

The veil between faith and medicine is both dense and transparent. The surgeon's conviction that Kevin would heal was made manifest in the room.

We believed.

When I arrived the next morning, tubes were neatly tied together rather than a sprawl of transparent plastic; a night nurse, during a quiet period, organized them while she and Kevin discussed gardens. This organization of tubes was reflective of a shift in Kevin, again the research scientist, utilizing all his problem-solving techniques. He and the surgeon established a plan of action which included cutting down on the morphine until he was free of it, possible because the inflammation had begun to dissipate. He would try first a bit of liquid, then slowly little bites of food until the paranutrition tube could be removed. I was overjoyed that he had again taken the reins of his life.

Within forty-eight hours Kevin weaned himself from morphine to Tylenol-3. He laboriously stood and pulling his IV pole of medicines and monitors, walked slowly down the hall beside me. He emailed scientists on his project, the head of his department, other project leaders and resumed work quarter-time from his bed. That day he sipped water and that evening took a few bites of Jello.

One morning, I woke up and realized that the snow had melted, crocuses poked spiny shoots from the ground and marsh marigolds pushed up through the mud of a tiny stream on our property. The sun was high and bright, infusing the air with spring warmth. I felt lighter, the falling away of winter a promise that our lives would be restored. Kevin was working on his computer when I arrived at the hospital. I paused a moment in the door, relieved at his color and at renewed industry he possessed.

"I checked with the nurses," I told him. "I'm going to take you outside. They've got a great little garden."

We carefully unplugged cords, wrapped them around the IV poles, put Kevin's jacket around his shoulders, and went out, settling onto a bench beneath a magnolia tree just beginning to bud. Daffodils were a blaze of gold, the green so fresh it dazzled. Hospital personnel passed, smiled, proclaimed it a beautiful day. Their casual greetings indicated nothing unusual about a man wearing baggy pajamas, a winter jacket, a wool sock hat, clutching a rod of hospital equipment, a tired woman beside him.

The seemingly endless day we'd been mired in had ended.

The next morning the feeding tube was removed.

The cause of Kevin's pancreatitis couldn't be determined, although his gall bladder was a possibility. Gall-stones can block the bile duct from the pancreas and cause inflammation. The surgeon suggested a procedure called ERCP in which a flexible tube is passed through the mouth to view the pancreatic ducts, yielding a great deal of information, but in rare instances inciting pancreatitis again. He left us alone to make our decision. While I favored the procedure, Kevin, shaken by the immense pain he'd experienced, refused to risk it. He asked to have his gall-bladder removed. The surgeon again indicated his preference for the ERCP, but respected Kevin's decision.

Three days after the arthroscopic surgery to remove his gall-bladder, Kevin came home. His brilliantly luminous return after a month in the hospital ended with another attack at 9:30 at night a few days later. I called the surgeon at home to tell him I was rushing Kevin to the hospital. He listened quietly, then said, "I'll call the hospital right now to get things rolling."

Things moved quickly. The surgeon had supported us in our gamble, but now insisted Kevin see Dr. X, an ERCP and pancreatic expert, at Maine Medical Center in Portland. He briefed Dr. X on Kevin's history, faxed all our records, then facilitated the transfer.

A week later, when some of the inflammation was under control Dr. X scheduled surgery. The morning of the operation we were quiet, frightened of what might be discovered, resolved to work around it and live our lives fully.

Dr. X discovered, and removed, a cyst occluding the sphincter that controls the duct from the pancreas to the duodenum. He felt the problem was resolved and while needing to be watched would most likely be OK.

This second return home from the hospital was far more subdued than the first, a lingering reminder that everything is transitory. At the end of Kevin's first week home, however, we had already begun to slip back into the normal rhythms of our lives, the hospital stay losing its immediacy. Kevin returned to work part-time, with a scheduled date for his full return. We took a walk through the nearby nature reserve. Our son's family visited bringing fruit and cards and relieved hugs. We all went to the movies and then out to eat. I puzzled about how the just-past can seem very long ago, how each day in the hospital seemed forever while here at home time vanished out from beneath us. What factor in human consciousness allows this distortion of time to occur, this lengthening and shortening of days even though each is twenty-four hours? How did we so quickly gain protective distance from what occurred?

I read once that during a crisis, strange and terrifying, we focus on every detail and this very focusing seems to slow time down. The more familiar things are, the less we take note of them and time flies past. For weeks after Kevin came home, however, there were certain hours when time became elastic again as my fear of Kevin's illness recurring, his fragility, my own aging, unspooled over endless nights, far longer than the days, and I tossed restlessly, torn between gratitude for the time given to us and fear of time's inevitable claws.

Stones

My husband, Kevin, and I recently spent an hour hunting for my mother's grave. It had been three years since we'd made the trip from Maine to New Jersey to visit the cemetery, and we had only vague memories of her gravesite's location. When we arrived, we picked up a detailed map from the cemetery office, which was decorated with thick carpets and wood paneling and staffed by older women in suits, heels, and fine jewelry. The woman behind the desk, eyeglasses perched low on her nose, searched through a large notebook labeled "G–I," then triumphantly announced, "Here it is: Jean Goodman." She marked the plot on the map with an X and drew a line from office to grave. "It's easy to find," she said, "just two rows behind the Ten Commandments."

We took the map and set out on foot rather than drive the labyrinth of roads crisscrossing the monument-covered landscape. The gray sky promised rain. Up ahead loomed the enormous marble tablets, like a prop in a Woody Allen film about God. By the time the shadow of the Commandments fell upon us, our sneakers were wet with dew.

Searching the long row for my mother's headstone was like seeking that particular tree in the forest into which you once carved a heart for somebody you loved. I strode impatiently back and forth over the drenched grass, rattling in my hand two rough stones that we'd brought from Maine, in keeping with the Jewish tradition of leaving stones on the grave to show that we had visited. They were striped rocks: white, gray, and black layers of a prehistoric past. I'd chosen them carefully from the various cairns of stones that rest in every corner of our house: on bathroom sinks, bureaus, the wood stove.

"I give up," I finally told Kevin. "We'll never find it. Let's leave the stones at the end of the row and start back before the rain starts."

Kevin, who's more patient than I am, wanted to give it one more try. Just then an elderly Hispanic man pulled up in a maintenance truck and asked if he could help. We handed him the map, and he searched intently, his brow wrinkled as he limped up the row. He finally paused, rubbed the grass with his shoe, and revealed metal. "Wait," he said and dashed off to his truck. A few moments later he returned with a shovel, carefully dug up the grassy soil, and exposed the plaque that marked my mother's grave:

Jean Goodman
Oct. 28, 1916 — May 14, 1982
feminist, beloved mother and grandmother

My mother had made all the arrangements for her funeral and burial, but she'd left it to me to compose the inscription on her plaque. When I'd handed a typed sheet of paper to the woman behind the counter at the monument company, she seemed charmed by what I'd written.

" 'Feminist,' " she said. "Imagine that."

"Yes," I said, "she was totally independent."

"So rare for a woman born in 1916."

I thought I detected a flash of envy in her eyes, and I realized she was probably the same age as my mother. She stared at the paper, as if lost in thought. I wondered what event in her life she was revisiting. Finally she looked up at me and asked, "Will you be buried in the same cemetery?"

I shook my head.

Kevin and I don't believe in funerals, burials, and gravestones. We plan to be cremated, attending to the commonplace business of dying with the least amount of rigmarole possible. I've asked my sons to scatter my ashes in New York City. When my daughter-in-law, an attorney, heard this, she told me she would research the legality of it, but as someone who grew up in a Brooklyn ghetto, I told her to just dump them without permission: considering the amount of debris on a Manhattan street, nobody would notice.

"You're not debris," she said.

"I'm not," I said, "but my body will be after I've left it."

Though my mother wanted to be buried, I believe that scattering her ashes hither and yon might have better suited her disposition. When her spirit departed her body, she was living in a tiny apartment in Newark, New Jersey, a city she had never thought of as home. She loved Manhattan, especially the hustling, noisy expanse of Second Avenue.

Depositing her ashes there would have been a fitting return.

I am the last living member of a family of three: my mother, my brother, and myself. (I never knew my father.) My brother was the first to die, killed in Vietnam. The military handled everything right down to the chilling refrain of Taps drifting across endless rows of identical white tombstones, symbol of a war that seemed equally endless. When my brother was alive, we'd never discussed death, avoiding any topic, really, that was likely to evoke feelings or involve family history. Actually, none of my friends' families discussed death either, ignoring its inevitability despite a lifetime of reminders. If we thought about it at all, we must have hoped we would stumble upon the right thing to do when our parents died. Studies suggest that elephants comfort their dying and caress their heads after they've passed. Is there some genetic predisposition in all creatures for mourning? If so, neither my mother nor I possessed that genetic legacy. When my brother was killed, my mother's howls were quickly silenced by an injection of sedative. After his burial, she remained silent and dry-eyed, giving up her beloved cigarettes as penance for the unnatural act of outliving her child. His death was rarely mentioned between us.

During my mother's funeral, I wandered the funeral parlor aimlessly, leaving my young sons to the care of close friends. I was grateful for the closed coffin and the brevity of the time her body would spend above ground: it's Jewish tradition to bury the dead within twenty-four hours. When

I'd seen her lifeless body in the hospital, I could hardly believe it was her. My animated, energetic mother had nothing in common with this stiff, mannequin-like form beneath the white hospital sheets. The vessel that had contained her spirit was as empty as the bottle of wine I later drank with my friends to toast her memory.

Though I think cemeteries deprive the living of needed space, some of them can be pleasant, parklike places. In Portland, Maine, historic Evergreen Cemetery is a massive swath of green that terminates at a pond inhabited by fat, contented ducks and geese. Visitors bring them stale-bread offerings, and the birds stay there year-round, through snow and freezing weather. I wander Evergreen frequently for exercise, silence, and history. I read the ancient inscriptions, admire the engravings and muse on the way names like Abigail, Charity, and Mabel go out of style, replaced by others that eventually suffer the same fate.

Evergreen's moss-laden mausoleums strike me as evidence of large and insecure egos, declaring the deceased's importance, but also acknowledging his or her fear of being forgotten. The dead, for the most part, do fade into obscurity: headstones are worn away; the last family members and acquaintances die. This fading seems necessary. Just as we must die to make room for the next generation, so must our memories dim. If we remembered every ancestor going back to Adam and Eve, there would be no room in our heads for the living.

Lately I've noticed something new at the cemetery: large

boxes made of Plexiglas that contain photographs — usually of teenagers or young adults — along with trophies, medals, baseballs, school awards, and various other memorabilia, like tiny museums devoted to a single individual. When I pass these transparent enclosures, I feel I've been handed a responsibility to join in the family's grieving process. Perhaps the families who erect these shrines are inviting cemetery visitors to bear witness to the unfairness of losing a loved one so young. The mementos strive to keep memories of the deceased as fresh and immediate as possible. But with the passage of time, memories become mere approximations of the people who are gone, no matter how hard we try to retain them. After thirty years I need to look at my mother's photograph to see her face clearly: the crow's feet; the plucked eyebrows; the humor in her eyes, and the sorrow behind that.

Lately, when driving on the highway, I've passed many white crosses commemorating those who have died in accidents, blue or pink ribbons waving in the wind from passing trucks. Sometimes several crosses are clustered at a particular spot, as though it were a kind of Bermuda Triangle where lives are sucked up in a screech of tires, brakes, and horns. These shrines serve as both memorials and cautionary statements. The white crosses remind me of military cemeteries, and I wish they too could be viewed by more of us as cautionary statements: this is what happens when we make war — our young vanish in a nightmare dreamed up by those who remain safe behind walls, alive and free to conjure up further destruction.

A few miles down the road from my house is a railroad track, and the other day, while waiting for the train to pass, I noticed a small white cross nearby. It was draped in fresh flowers, but the death couldn't have been recent, or I would have read about it. Also, the paint on the cross was peeling. How had this particular death occurred? A suicide? A stalled truck? A vehicle that lost its race with a train? The fresh flowers were evidence of ongoing grief. Whoever had brought them needed to go to a florist, drive to the site, step carefully between the trestles, and scramble up a pebble-laden embankment to leave the roses. This little monument has served its purpose: I can no longer pass the train track without recognizing that somebody lost his or her life there, and caution is required. Thinking of the Jewish tradition, I imagine thousands of little stones surrounding the cross, each representing a visit from a person in a passing car or train.

I also live near an old cemetery atop a steep hill, and I climbed up there one morning to examine the slate headstones. Most were no longer readable, their edges worn away and ragged, like the decaying teeth of an ancient giant. There are many such cemeteries scattered throughout Maine. A friend told me about walking some overgrown land he was considering buying and discovering a small family cemetery made impenetrable by thorny masses of wild roses. Worn gravestones lay on their sides, shrouded by grass and bushes. My friend was dismayed, but I found it a lovely thought: wild roses embracing the forgotten gravesites, the earth reclaiming everything. I recalled a line from a Carl Sandburg poem: *"I am the grass; I cover all."*

My husband is a scientist, and four years ago I accompanied him to an environmental conference in Japan. Our hosts were eager to show us the Japan most tourists never see, and we spent a couple of days on a bus, visiting out-of-the-way locales. Our last stop was a sulfurous location whose name translates loosely as Wounded Rock. The almost-viscous odor swirled around us. Our eyes watered; our throats stung. I thought of the fire-and-brimstone hell conjured by old-time preachers.

But once we climbed over the slope, we forgot about the stench. We were looking out upon thousands of hand-carved statues called "jizo," deities who pray for travelers. Each wore a decaying red bib and head scarf sewn by local women to symbolize impermanence. Wounded Rock has long been a destination for Japanese spiritual pilgrims. Many died traveling there on foot over the centuries, leaving their families back home uncertain whether to issue prayers for the dead. Local craftsmen carved a jizo for each dead pilgrim, so that he or she might be eternally prayed for.

Though there were no remains at Wounded Rock, it felt like a burial ground. I wandered slowly among the statues, which comforted me with their apparent message that the death we all travel to meet is not so frightening.

That day at Wounded Rock was also the anniversary of my mother's death. Our hosts had told us that visitors to the site place stones beside the jizo to remember their own dead.

Stunned by the similarity to the Jewish ritual and by the serendipity of our being there on that particular date, I honored my mother by placing a stone at the feet of a small jizo whose hands were raised in prayer and eyes were closed in meditation.

I can't picture myself dying. The actual process — with all its uncertainly about when, where, and how — is too much to contemplate. I can, however, imagine the moment after death: a quiet state, perhaps close to what we sometimes achieve during meditation; the absence of fear, worry, hate, and anger. Or maybe there is only emptiness. As an atheist, I find it both disquieting and comforting to think that there is nothing else after the body has ceased to function. But Einstein proved that energy never vanishes, so there is also the possibility of my energy circling the places I loved and the lives of my children and grandchildren.

I collect seashells, old turtle shells, fossils, sand dollars, pieces of wood, bleached bones — the cast-off remains of once-living things. They remind me that dying is universal, the most ancient certainty, both revered and feared. Even stars die, blasting their light across the dark universe. Each of us follows in the footsteps of countless others who have gone before us; death is the final equalizer between each human and between humans and other species. I don't dwell on death, but I know I'm past the midpoint of my days. My life is a vessel steadily emptying.

Like my mother, I've made arrangements for what will happen to my body after death. Unlike her, I'll have no headstone, only the stones I have brought back to our house from my travels. I need no more monument than the slice of lava from Herculaneum in Italy; the magically flat stone from Kyoto, Japan; the vivid red rock from New Mexico. I'm humbled to have possessed them for a brief span of their long existence. I can imagine my sons handling their smooth curves and worn edges as they think of me after I'm dead, until finally they, too, are gone, and only the stones remain.

Roses at the End of Summer

"My life is leaking out of me like..." She holds up the hose she is using to water her plants and wiggles it at me. "Like the water is leaking out of this garden hose." My expression makes clear my reluctance to surrender hope. She shakes her head and says with a toughness that she has only recently developed, "Shape up. You don't have much time left to reach that desired stage of acceptance."

She lifts the hose to her lips to drink. Water drizzles down her chin and comes to rest in a shimmering pendant against her throat. She grimaces, "Rubbery," tosses it to the ground, and a widening rainbow begins to arch around the nozzle. This adroit process of capturing and decoding color from sunlight also captures my friend's attention. She watches the transformation of water, grass, air into some glistening new thing.

"Transformation" has begun to appear with regularity in her conversation, along with the word "meditation," and stillness has replaced the restlessness that's marked her for as long as we've been friends. I watch her for a few moments. She's very slender now, the sturdiness that marked her frame whittled down, then feeling as though I'm somehow spying on a private moment, I stretch out on a lounge chair shaded by a sugar maple in blazing regalia, and close my eyes.

Despite the dry autumn the grass is lush. My friend waters diligently, mourning each flowering annual as its season for life passes. Russet and gold have overtaken much of the soft green of summer, but mums spike purple, yellow and white in her raised beds. Three of her rose bushes are studded with tiny hard hips, prepared for winter, "the little death" but the fourth, a cottage rose, in stubborn disregard of the cold nights, is flooded with pink buds even as the petals of spent blossoms curl brown and drop. The tenacity of the bush delights her and she feeds it against all advice that it should be encouraged to go quietly dormant.

"We're in a race," she said when I arrived. "Which of us will hold out the longest." She cocked her head at my silence and said, "Get with it." Her eyes were hard. I knew then that she was going to be relentless.

She trembles a moment, then walks to the side of the house where the faucet is. The hose offers a final hissing spurt, the spreading rainbow stalled. In just a few minutes, the earth will absorb the water and the rainbow will vanish. I close my eyes and try to meditate using a mantra she gave me, an experience she insisted I'd love, but my mind scurries through problems with my psychotherapy clients, the book I'm writing, my husband's upcoming business trip. The lounge chair beside me shifts and I open my eyes. She's moved it into the late morning sun and rests there now, with closed eyes. Her pale face is slathered with sunblock. Her hipbones jut against her dark jeans. Her hair has grown back in the short silver curls of Roman boys in old frescoes.

"Should you move out of the sun?" I ask.

She shakes her head. "I'll have lots of time to be in the dark."

★

I'd stocked my car with Maine icons for this visit; soap and moisturizer from Tom's of Maine, photographs of the coast, apples, maple syrup, a ceramic crow from a gallery in Portland, an L.L.Bean vest, and a poster from the Portland Museum of Art. In honor of our history of junk-shopping, I brought an exotic gypsy scarf, gaudy dangling earrings, six mystery books and two cashmere sweaters from the Salvation Army.

My husband watched as I layered it all onto my back seat and said, "Hug her for me." I nodded. He hesitated after kissing me good-bye, then added, "Tell her I'll see her soon."

I nodded again, but we both knew it was a crapshoot.

She ran out to the driveway when I arrived, then glowed when I threw open the car's back door and began to fill her arms with my gifts.

"That's all?" she said. "Are you sure you didn't forget anything?"

★

Three days have passed, only two left before I leave, and my face in the mirror is drawn, the fine web of lines deeper, eyes already speaking the language of loss. Time is slipping out from under me. "Why her?" I whispered to my reflection. My mother, brother, my first husband's grandparents and aunt, two other friends and a writer who was an acquaintance are all dead; also, Miles Davis, Francois Truffaut, Raymond Carver, Andrew Dubus, Billie Holiday, Janis Joplin, Jimi Hendrix, millions known and unknown. Nobody survives life.

I stretched, sighed at the throb of my aging knees after running on the hard pavement and took a hot shower. Over breakfast, my friend ate a last spoonful of oatmeal and examined me. "You look like shit."

"Thanks," I answered. "I'm going to meditate on that."

She laughed and said, "Let's go sit in the yard after I water."

My friend opens her eyes and looks at my watch. "Time to go." She stands in a single, graceful motion and I realize she's been practicing to move as though she's still a healthy woman. She threw her watch in the trash when she learned she was dying. "Time is a concept devoid of meaning," she said. "A day with my children is shorter than a second, a twenty-minute wait for the results of a test is longer than a year, and dying will take as long as it takes."

After dinner each night, we watch reruns of her favorite shows. In the darkness of the living room, as images flicker across the screen, time accordions back into itself, Alan Alda maturely handsome rather than time-ravaged, William Shatner not yet camp, Red Skelton's drunk act funny before we acknowledged the effects of alcoholism. We are sealed into a twenty-five-year old time capsule, a long-ago time when only other people died. Time - I read an article on how we really don't know what it is, and that it actually does move faster and slower. If we figure out the system we can be in any time at all. I don't understand the theory.

My friend beckons from beside the cottage rose where she waits for me to get my car keys. "Let's go. I don't have forever." Her finger and toenails are polished the same shocking pink as the roses, a smooth vibrancy that radiates like waves in the air around her. She flashed her fingernails at me when I first arrived, then pointed to her polished toes in the sandals she wore despite the chilly day, and said, "We're having a girly party later and I'm polishing yours."

Our friendship began as young mothers and she's offering an opportunity to experience a makeshift adolescence together, a flight to a past that we didn't share, "OK," I agreed, hauling my suitcase from the trunk. "Polish away, except I refuse to watch Gidget and drink Coke while you do it."

"Stop dawdling," she says now as I carry the lounge chairs to her porch.

"It might rain," I protest.

She shakes her head at my compulsivity and asks, "Where? In India?"

She bends to sniff one of the roses. Pain floods her face and she rests her hand against the curve of her back. My throat knots with sorrow. She looks up to hurry me, sees my face and quickly plunges her nose back into the petals.

I clear my throat and say, "Let's go."

175

When we're belted into the car she turns to me, squares her shoulders and challenges, "Now?"

I nod and we grab the handles that open our windows.

"OK," she says. "Ready, set, go."

She churns passionately and opens her window first, then clasps her hands above her head in a gesture of triumph. "Winner and still champion. You buy lunch - again."

"This time." I start the car, back out, and turn into the road.

"Ha," she scoffs and leans out the window. The brim of her stained green cap, one her garage mechanic gave her when she admired it, snaps in the wind. As the car picks up speed, she pulls her head back to answer, "You're running out of time to win." Through the window the American suburbs race behind her like a video on fast forward.

Relentless, I think, then answer, "There's the trip back home."

"No," she says quietly. "We both know I'm gonna be first." She leans out the window, but not before I catch a glimpse of her eyes.

In the oncologist's office, we wait for her examination. Vapid watercolors interrupt the long expanse of walls painted blue and pink like a baby's nursery. Closed blinds block every window and thin rods of light sneak in and rest along the flat beige carpet. The radio plays music you forget even as you hear it. The only other patient is a man who sits across from us restlessly fingering an issue of The New Yorker. He's gaunt, with eyes like the last lingering coals of a fire, dressed in a crisp white shirt and paisley tie. A heavy sweater and fedora rest beside him and his grey hair is the cropped length of new spring grass. His mouth is wry and humorous and a little bitter.

She cocks her head at the radio and says, "Steely Dan would drop dead if they heard this version of Dr. Wu." She puts down a magazine and smiles at the man who'd laughed at her comment and now grins at us.

"So, is this where you come to loosen up?" she says and I realize, by the tone of her voice, that she's flirting.

"Yes, and what's a nice girl like you doing in a place like this?" he flirts back. He's wearing a wedding band. So is my friend.

"Where else can you get a cocktail with this kind of kick?" she answers and shimmies her shoulders provocatively.

I'm astonished, then further surprised to see him shimmy back with a quick self-conscious movement. His name is called and he rises, making a drinking motion with his cupped hand, pretending to stagger as the door to the doctor's office softly closes behind him.

My friend burps noisily, as though she's had too much to drink and the receptionist looks up from her desk to smile vacantly into the almost empty room.

"I should have at least one affair before I die," she says, then adds, "Some kind of affair, anyway." She sighs but her eyes gleam.

"Hey." I swallow hard and glance at her shocking nails. "We've only got one life to live." Her laugh tells me I said the right thing. It's getting both easier and harder to accomplish that.

She fidgets as time drags on and whispers loudly, "Who

has all this time to kill?" The receptionist's eyes blink rapidly but she doesn't look up. My friend stares out the window and I memorize her profile. I miss her already. First marriages, children, my younger son's surgery, divorces, present marriages, I imagine it impossible for an event to occur in my life if she's not there to witness it. She turns to me and I look quickly out the window.

"I felt that," she says.

I shake my head and ask, "Where is all this telepathy coming from?"

"I'm practicing channeling," she answers. "First on the receiving end, later on the sending."

"Are you going to be this relentless the whole trip?"

"It depends on you," she says. "It may need to be the whole trip."

The magazine she put down lies open at a quiz: "Do you have the courage to dream big?"

"Let's take it," I say.

We scoff at each inane question about decorating your house, choosing your car, changing make-up. There's a gravity to the phrasing of each question that suggests meticulous attention to external trappings is essential for psychic harmony. The final question is, "Are you excited about every new adventure?"

"I lose," my friend says and closes the magazine.

I experience a moment of vertigo at the bleakness in her voice and grab her hand just as the doctor's door opens and the man steps out buttoning the sleeves of his shirt. He's paler than when he went in and looks around as though uncertain of where he is until he sees my friend and smiles.

He sits down and says, "I need to wait in case I have a reaction to the injection."

The nurse gestures that it's my friend's turn, and as she passes him, one long leg brushes his knee and she says, "That's all you're waiting for?"

I catch my breath at her unfamiliar boldness then look at the clean, worn angles of his face and something inside me cheers.

His eyes lighten and he answers, "Maybe not all."

He watches her vanish behind the closed door, turns to me and nods. We smile at each other and I'm suddenly self-conscious about my fingernails, as though I haven't earned the right to their brave shade of pink.

We sit silently, me turning the pages of a magazine, him watching the play of light on the carpet, until my friend swings open the door of the doctor's office, says something quietly over her shoulder then closes the door behind her. She sees the man, inhales sharply, then asks, "No bad reaction?"

"Oh, that," he says. "I forgot about that. I'm just hanging out soaking up the ambiance."

Her smile is brilliant and she leans over, her hand on his shoulder and asks, "Can you tear yourself away from the music and join us for lunch?"

He immediately stands, pulls his sweater over his head, adjusts the fedora, and cocks an arm at each of us. "Let's go. I'm dying of hunger."

My friend laughs and takes his arm. "We're going to a little organic restaurant I love."

"Perfect," he says, waving his elbow at me again and I take it.

Outside, a milky scarf of clouds drifts across the sky. The sun is demanding and bitterly bright for so late in the season.

"I'll follow you," he says, opens his car door and slides in. "Drive slowly."

I nod and my friend pats his hand on the steering wheel. He looks at her and there is something so stark and naked on his face that I look away.

"It's on this road," I mumble. "Just about ten miles on the right-hand side."

"I'll follow you," he says again.

Once we're on the road, she watches his car in the rear-view mirror, leans her head out the window, waves, then sits back in her seat. When I stop at a red light, she applies lipstick and pats on face power, pursing her lips at how dry and flaky her skin is. I feel my heart break.

We eat winter squash soup and endive salad at a table beneath a picture window. Sun filters gently through gauze curtains. The restaurant is quiet. We're between the lunch and dinner hours. Each table has a small rose and when we first sat down my friend leaned over to sniff then said with disappointment, "They're scentless."

"You like roses?" the man asked.

"I love them," she said. "I have one still putting out blossoms like it hasn't figured out we've shifted to mid-autumn."

"A fighter," he answers.

Throughout the meal, they laugh and speak in tongues, a complex language of medications, treatments and experimental programs that is beyond my capacity to fluently converse in. It's not a graceful or smooth dialect, yet they speak it as though it were a romance language. She eats with more interest than I've seen for a while, nodding enthusiastically and waving her fork in the air to make a point. He's pushed his bowl and plate away and rests his face on his palms watching her, laughing when she says something funny, nodding when she says something serious.

They begin to talk about their lives before…

He insists they have a lot in common. She was an editor in her "former life" and he's an avid reader. She's addicted to computers - "Naturally," she flashes her eyes at him - and he was a science teacher. They both love museums. His wife owns a business and travels all the time, and since my friend received what she calls her "sentence," her husband works late and on weekends and is always at a conference somewhere.

"He's buying new suits and watching his diet," she says.

She takes another forkful of salad, then pushes her plate up beside his.

He nods silently.

Her mouth twists as she grabs my hand and says, "He and I have both grown thinner although not together. By now I hardly miss him."

He looks at us with an ancient sadness, also with the satisfaction of the old friend he has somehow become. His eyes mirror an elemental loneliness that traverses both the living and the dying, although they are really the same. He reaches across the table and squeezes both our hands for a moment. I'm a little bit in love with him myself, the aplomb with which he's revealed himself.

They discover more commonalities. They both use sparingly their sleeping pills and painkillers. They both refused a second round of chemotherapy, believing it's not worth the misery just to get a few more months of struggle. They muse over the role of alternative therapy in America and discover, to their mutual delight, that they both follow a regime of vitamins and herbs prescribed by the same neighborhood naturopath.

"Hell," my friend says, "I've never felt better in my life." She leans toward him seductively, a vestigial mannerism from a time when she still had breasts. Leaves tremble outside the window and shadows flicker over her like candlelight.

He nods, leaning forward also. "I don't believe you've ever looked more beautiful."

Their fingers meet across the table. There is something glowing inside her that I haven't seen for a few years, a feverish light that ignites her. She is "transformed." I know she would laugh derisively at me because I imagine a miracle, things beyond medical science.

We order coffee and she takes hers with cream, a luxury she never allowed herself before. She and I get chocolate cake. He gets apple pie. They exchange tastes of their desserts. There is a field around them of mid-afternoon haze and shadows, their skin translucent as rice paper, blue veins delicate as map lines. Everything is surreal, slowed down. It takes an hour for the pie-laden fork he holds up to reach her lips. It takes as long for her hand to touch his.

He insists on paying the bill. "Our first date," he jokes, then turns to generously include me.

Outside they exchange telephone numbers. The trees transform sunlight into a cool green that drops over us. Russet leaves drift down onto the grass. There is a massive bush of cottage roses on each side of the restaurant entrance and while hips have taken over, a few blossoms remain, flooding the air with their fragrance. The man swoops and plucks one, carefully avoiding the thorns and presents it to my friend who bows gracefully in gratitude. They graze cheeks then he leans over to kiss me as well. "See you," he says.

I answer honestly, "I hope so."

He walks to his car waving over his shoulder. His shoulders are broad, his walk a little stiff but still fluid; a man traveling a path between the middle and old age of a terminal disease. My friend watches him, one finger caressing the soft petals, inadvertently loosening a few which fall to the path. "Beautiful," she says and I nod.

She rolls her window down before I'm even in the car and I settle into my seat protesting, "Hey, not fair."

"Sometimes, you've just gotta cheat," she tells me then leans out of the window as the car picks up speed.

When we arrive at the house she laughs at the lounge chairs folded neatly on the porch and holds her palm out mockingly. I'm preparing herb tea when her husband calls from D.C. where he's attending a conference. She holds the cordless phone in one hand, and with her other grabs a spoon and plays a row of glasses on the counter.

"Nothing's changed," she tells him, shaking her head. "No, nothing's worse and nothing's better." She's quiet... then, "No, had lunch with a man we met at the doctor's office, the three of us." She's quiet again then stares directly into my eyes and says briskly, as though reciting a weather report, "Same as mine, hopeless." A muscle twitches in her jaw. My heart pounds so hard I have tunnel vision and drop to a chair. After a moment of silence, she says, "OK, OK," and the spoon speeds up, alternating between glasses. "Nothing," she says and stops. "Some noise from outside." After another moment she tells him, "No, don't call. I'll be asleep by then." She plays the glasses again, gently, a paled symphony of crystal instruments. "Yes, good-by."

She hangs up and turns to me, "Bastard," she says. "He's getting impatient."

We're in the yard, wrapped in light blankets, drinking tea and watching the sun surrender the sky when the phone rings. She goes in to get it. Her eyes are thoughtful when she returns and asks, "Would you mind if I went out for a while this evening?" The blazing sunset transforms her to a dark silhouette, a brilliant aura of fiery orange flaring around her.

"Uh-oh," I stand and put my hand on my forehead in feigned shock and say, "A date. Do I know this boy? Don't get into a car if the driver has been drinking."

"I promise," she says quietly, then takes a few steps forward and her arms fiercely encircle me. I feel her tears against my cheek as she trembles violently, great shuddering waves of the terror she cradles inside. I rub her back and think of her husband, growing more absent and remote. I hate him then and know he is no longer a part of this equation except in the concrete abstract, if that makes any sense. She has friends who love her, women who will rally around her, do anything she needs, but there are needs that we can't meet. She is counting on the man and he is probably counting on her. Time has collapsed like a building falling into itself and what would take weeks in ordinary time has transpired in an afternoon.

I'm terrified then...I want her to die first. I don't want her to suffer his vanishing, be left behind to wait for her own entry into infinity.

I've reached acceptance at last.

"Is this a good idea?" I whisper to her.

"Because I'm married?" she asks bitterly.

"No."

She steps away from me, grabs my hands, and studies my face. She nods.

"Yes," she says. "You're finally there. And yes, it's a good idea."

I feel an unexpected flash of jealousy when her car pulls out of the driveway a half-hour later. I promised her I'd try to meditate again, but I can't still myself and wander around her house. I touch things as familiar to me as my own: the old table we found at a yard sale during a walk and lugged home, carrying it between us, putting it down every few minutes, asking ourselves, "Why don't we get the car," and then lifting it again. I run my fingers over a Navaho pot my husband and I bought her when we were in New Mexico, the reds seeming to float over the tan background. There's a ridiculous crystal chandelier we found at GoodWill that was missing the parts to hang it. We scoured second hand stores and finally, in a stroke of genius, she balanced it carefully in an enormous glass vase. There's a photograph taken when we were both still married to our first husbands. Our faces are earnest, unlined - a still shot of time before the world crashed in on us.

There are old books I own as well: *Play It as It Lays, The Wanderer, Will You Please Stop Talking, Please,* and new ones resting beside them; *A Path with Heart, Peace is Within, Transformation and Meditation,* all dog-eared and well used. Then there are her records, also identical to mine: the four Nick Drake LP's, John Martin, Miles Davis, John Coltrane, a Tiny Tim I gave her as a gag gift, Bob Dylan. The Marvin Gaye LP resurrects a Halloween party where we wore spangled clothing and harmonized, badly, on "What's going on?" When I find a Madonna, all hard body and fuck-me eyes, I'm astonished, then not, then laugh loudly finally breaking into gasping sobs. I sink onto her couch, grateful to be alone at this moment. The pain is relentless, every crevice of self-deceit sealed. I walk from room to room crying, knowing that when she is gone I will never see these rooms, these things again. Her vanishing will suck in everything after it, a vacuum that will consume everything of her that is not in my possession.

Afterward, I pour a glass of wine. My body is edgy, my mind a whirling kaleidoscope. I can't read. I change into nightclothes, climb into bed with a second glass of wine and click on the television. There's a rerun of Star Trek. I want to be "beamed" somewhere, to disappear into a reality where anything is possible. I plump up the pillows and settle down. I don't remember what else I watched, laying awake listening anxiously for her to come home. Don't be an idiot, I admonish myself. An automobile accident would be too much of a weird irony. I finally sleep.

My friend is drinking coffee at the kitchen table, a bouquet of roses in the center. She smiles up at me when I kiss the top of her head. There's a relaxed softness to the fine, high cheekbones and a luminosity to her skin. She seems younger in the gentle morning light, the woman I'd met when we were twenty-something's. I have been briefly "beamed" back to a time that lingers somewhere. I pour a cup of coffee, sniff the roses, sit down and take her hand.

"You had fun?" I ask, although it's rhetorical.

She nods and her smile is shy, a girl's. "When was the last time you sat up half the night talking and necking and making stupid jokes?" she asks dreamily.

"Too far back in the primordial to remember." I take a sip of coffee.

My friend giggles at something she remembers and the sound is so delightful that I giggle also. She takes my hand and there's fear in her eyes, but something else also - a brief staying power that has made time bend in some crazy, forgiving way, a Mobius strip with no beginning and no end.

Last year, in a phone conversation, she said wistfully, "I miss passion most of all." I was silent for a few minutes and then said lamely, "There're different kinds of passion." She laughed and answered, "Ever the therapist." Passion. She is not experiencing the frantic carnality of young adulthood, or the comfortable familiarity of middle-aged partners. It is the thrilling teen-age experience of crushes and kisses and handholding.

Long ago, in a workshop on death, the woman seated beside me worked in hospice. She raised her hand and said, "It always seems, to me anyway, like time begins to move backward, that people who are dying become middle-aged, then younger, then babies, until finally, death is like birth." My friend is traveling along the road of time, the past, the present, the future melting. Memories of long ago are happening even as we remember them. I am meditating, finally, my mantra a chant for mercy, and she is so alive, so present, her smile so radiant that I stop time right there.

Winter

Winter blasts us with four blizzards nearly back-to-back. Snow explodes - avalanches tumbling from a sullen sky. By mid-afternoon, opaque waves of white render every other color obsolete: a sort of snow blindness. Swift sheets of wind shape fleeing ghosts that haunt corners and circle trees. The snow provides its own brightness, sucking up residual sunlight and beaming it back to us like a flat, cold sun.

We're prepared: split wood columned beside the woodstove, a can of maple syrup for sugar on snow, flashlights in every room. Kevin, my husband, has a stack of New Yorker Magazines. I am reading a book on the Inuit, a culture inseparable from, and reliant upon, winter. The Inuit word for winter is ukivq, which is also the word for year and the long Maine winter can indeed feel like a year. The Inuit consider extreme conditions and the lengthy absence of daylight a time for dreaming, storytelling, communicating with the spirits, as if the distraction of sunlight obfuscates clarity. It is an enviable purity similar to the Buddhist philosophy of seeing the world as it is and finding the joy in it.

The fire crackles, spits sparks of red and blue, the air

redolent with burning wood. Our house, a warm cave carved into the cold, has grown a shell of snow. I rest my fingers against the flake-dusted window that reflects my transparent face, turbulence whirling behind it as though some spirit wind moves though me. Pines jitterbug to a fierce melody. Chickadees dart at birdfeeders then soar away as though snatched by the wind. I remove my fingers from the glass, their frosty shape gradually fading like an old photograph in too much light.

There is never a day that we don't go out. The Inuit word, Sila, roughly translates as the breath of the world, consciousness, weather and so much more. Kevin and I need Sila, need that breath. In late afternoon, we dress in snowsuits, strap on snowshoes, battle the wind for control of the door and go out. A merciless gust steals my breath. Stiffness seizes me as though my limbs are frozen. The air vibrates, a wind instrument playing a tuneless scale. We shoe across the backyard into the woods where we're sheltered by pine and hemlock, branches bowed beneath the snowy weight. The orange flagging Kevin tied to individual trees to mark a path is hidden by snow that has caterpillared up tree trunks. We look for landmarks, but there has been a shift, the familiar and unfamiliar residing in each other. We have been relocated to a country of ephemera: growing mounds of snowdrifts, miniature hills birthing on tree boughs, newly recorded animal markings that vanish even as we watch. Kevin brushes tree-trunks with a gloved hand, seeking flags with little success and we concentrate, instead, on plowing through the white world around us.

Thick layers cover our boots and threaten the theft of our

snowshoes, our journey narrated by snowshoe tracks splayed out behind us. Just as birds ate Hansel and Gretel's breadcrumbs, the falling snow will eat our tracks. I scale rising drifts by grasping tree trunks, quickly drenched with perspiration beneath my jacket and snowpants. Even my fingers and toes, originally protesting the ten-degree temperature with numbness, are comfortable.

There is a joke in Maine; if you don't like the weather, wait five minutes, but this year's contrasts have been startling. The preceding week brought fifty to fifty-five degree temperatures, broke weather records and deposited a false patina of spring. Kevin and I strolled nearby Ogunquit, a tourist town mostly shuttered in winter. Visitors, giddy in the January thaw, bought hot chocolate and donuts from one of the few open shops. Kevin, a research scientist whose work involves trees and global climate change, paused to examine prematurely sprouting pussy willows, those furry precursors of spring.

"Nearly two months early," he said, running his fingers over the buds.

The willows were not alone in their confusion as to what season it was: oak and maple buds were swelling, the sharp tips of daffodils poking through layers of slushy ice. We walked between two closed hotels to reach Marginal Way, a cliff walk mobbed with natives taking advantage of the warmth, a few teenagers in Bermuda shorts, most of us wearing sneakers rather than boots. Strangers greeted each other with "Beautiful day." The cliff path winding along the ocean was alternately puddled or icy as snow from the previous week had repetitively melted and froze. We'd all regressed to clumsy toddlers as we gingerly navigated patches of ice. The ocean smacked the cliffs with thick veils of white foam as waves lifted and dropped with unrestrained power. The sky was the flat blue of blown glass and temporarily cloudless. I understood the perils of global climate change, yet couldn't help feeling energized after a week of shrouded skies, perleroneg, the sense of being crazed by extended darkness, vanquished.

The sun's rose-tinged descent by four o'clock seemed incongruous with the spring weather, as though the warmth could somehow extend daylight. We headed home, reluctant to let go of the day. Our son called just as we got there, told us about taking his daughters, two-year-old Sadie and four-year-old Ceiligh, out to the park near his house. I spoke briefly to each as they informed me, with some sadness, that their snowman had melted. I told them that the opportunity to build other snowman was likely. The following morning the temperature dropped sharply and snow pounded us as though revenging the warmth of the previous days.

★

Those soaring temperatures had encouraged the formation of vernal pools in our woods way ahead of their traditional spring arrival. The Inuit call spring immaturpuq, "when the Earth receives its first water," and vernal pools, "the first water" are spring's welcome harbingers, amoebic-like sacs of snowmelt that nourish various species from infancy to adulthood. We struggled to avoid stepping into these thinly iced bowls even as they sucked snow down their sides like quicksand, splitting the ground into snaking ditches. Again and again we encountered narrow streams widening into miniature lakes, sometimes plunging into them as the snow caved beneath our feet.

There seemed a literary quality to this juxtaposition of winter and spring crammed together, how the fiery heat of snow against my cheeks echoed July sun, a reminder of the smooth flow of the seasons. I marveled at how nature had perfected a continuum carefully balanced to sustain life, each season's process one of death and rebirth: spring laboriously conquering winter, summer's abundance running rampant over spring, autumn's blazing take-down of summer, winter's shortened days forcing life underground, then the expanding light of spring renewing the cycle. Kevin and I have watched the growing disruptions with dismay. Autumnal breaks in summer with forty-degree weather that incites premature senescence in trees; spring-like fissures in winter, rising temperatures waking buds that will freeze in the plunge back to frigidity; seasonal havoc occurring more frequently and more intensely each passing year.

Late afternoon's last gasping bursts of ivory heralded the end of the latest storm. The yard was a pale lunarscape that ran into the darkness of the woods. The austerity of this rippled white deepened the greened density just beyond. The rising boulders of our ancient granite quarry had morphed into a sprawl of something softer, rounder. Winter in Maine is not just a season but a location, sign-posted in layers of cold-white drifts and gritty ice.

Kevin went outside to snow-blow the driveway while I

raked the roof of the woodshed beside our buried deck, the raked snow contributing to the mountain that made roof and deck a single level. When I was done, I sat on the snow-mountain and admired the variegated shades of soft gray that quilted the sky. The cold was so intense that breathing seemed an aerobic activity, yet peace had taken hold. The wind had stopped its moaning and quiet was its own sound, although it's never really quiet. There's the rapid run of a squirrel up a tree, the flap of chickadees at the birdfeeder, the marauding wind through the spruce and pine. Once when I visited a friend in central Maine who lived near a frozen lake, we listened to the ringing, humming, groaning of cracking ice as the afternoon passed.

"The Earth speaking," he told me with glowing face; remembering that I think, Sila.

By the time Kevin and I went inside to eat dinner, it was fully dark. Clouds obfuscated evening light, landscape indistinct in the absence of moon and stars. This blurry vista, sometimes occurring after a blizzard, has always appeared apocalyptic to me, a reminder of how fragile and yet resilient everything is and of how carelessly we challenge that resilience.

I looked out at the camouflaging layers, knowing there would be more to come. Snow sometimes remains on the ground well into spring. One May I flew home from California and looked down at a patchwork of white, green and brown. That lingering snow is one reason winter feels a year long, yet snow is vital to the ecology of Maine, indeed to all snow-laden areas. It is a blanket that insulates life germinating underground. The year we had little snow and frigid temperatures, half our garden plants didn't return, crops suffered, and there was a shortage of food for migrating birds.

In the middle of the night I was woken by wind that had returned with renewed ferocity. It circled the house like a growling dog. I opened my eyes to an incandescent glow; the room's contents hued in hazy silver. It was cold, the wood stove long out, and I shivered as I walked to the window, which framed a startlingly bright full moon, the snow beneath it a spill of soft opalescence. Shadows crept across the yard like scurrying animals as the wind seized everything it could. Oaks and maples, reduced to their essential skeletons in winter, were bathed in pearled-white. Fleeing clouds scrolled a manuscript of sharp white stars out behind them. An owl flew by, its shadow looming over a scurrying rodent that vanished behind the snowbound rock wall. The deep moans of the wind seeped in as if by osmosis. Wind and trees engaged in a battle of strength as the wind furiously shook the trees. I knew that by daylight a few would not have survived the assault.

The temperature the next morning was minus four and the air seemed fragile as crystal, as if it might shatter from the mere act of moving though it. The sun shed pale gold over the trees, their shadows wavering columns across the yard. The radio spoke of unusually cold air. I pulled on a heavy sweater, lined jeans, and wool socks then went downstairs. Kevin, awake earlier than usual, had lit the wood stove and made coffee. As I poured myself a cup he opened the door, bundled in high boots, thick jacket, pants over thermal underwear. His eyes were watery, nose red, boots crusted with snow. He pulled off his gloves, flexed his fingers then cupped them around a cup of coffee I handed him.

"I have to leave for work in a minute, I just wanted to see what fell last night; mostly softwoods. We may have to cut an oak for next winter if one doesn't come down over the next few months."

Next winter, I thought, we're still in the middle of this one. But then, sometimes winter seems the only season, briefly punctuated by warmth. We prepare for it no matter where we are in the calendar. After a blizzard, Kevin chainsaws downed trees we'll use for the following winter. Once snow melts in late spring, we pile them onto our wheelbarrow and pull them to an old oak stump where he'll split each log. Through summer and autumn, Kevin splits wood that we haul and stack in the woodshed. We gather branches and twigs for kindling, buy mulch to cover plants, repair storm windows damaged by rodents or rot, check ice scrapers, snow blowers, heaters. I don't want to plan for next winter in the midst of this one, but I'm already mulling over next year as though time has fast-forwarded.

Kevin kisses me goodbye, his car vanishing behind snow corridors piled high along the road by the snowplow. I stare out at the sprawling terrain and the house grows cramped. I eat a bowl of oatmeal as I watch birds swoop and dip into the pool of water created by our sump pump, then leave my dish in the sink, pull on mittens, jacket and snowshoes and slide down the slope of snow-curved steps. My face stings.

My toes complain. My breath fans out behind me so thickly that I imagine it a contrail too dense to evaporate. I shoe into the woods striped by thin ribbons of light that christen treetops with brightness and offer a broken path of radiance. Everything shimmers, a thousand shafts of sun like a fire in the snow. I pass between trees as if through doorways, slide down small hills, find my way around the vernal pools packed with leaves and lichen-dressed twigs pressed beneath ice like cloudy glass. I kneel to peer in at a complicated sculpture of lacy green lichen, rough brown twigs, curling russet leaves, white birch bark. The sun moves overhead and my shadow is suddenly part of the sculpture, reminding me that in some Inuit dialects, the word for man is interchangeable with the word for shadow.

There is an Inuit word, ablautseneq: corporeal and perceptual transformation. Traditional Inuit believed that a shaman could shape-shift into any animal, described in the poem Magic Words: "Sometimes they were people, and sometimes animal, and there was no difference. They all spoke the same language." In Western culture, that concept is alien, but here in the woods I want to believe in the possibility; I want to be a fox I once saw flying across the snow. I stand and begin to shoe again. An earlier history has been written beneath my feet on snow parchment; bird, deer, domestic cats, dogs and coyote tracks. My own, created by wide, multi-squared plastic, dissolve any fantasy of ablautseneq; I am only a middle-aged, American white woman.

I have become so immersed in my musings that I paid no attention to last night's faint snowshoe tracks and find myself lost. I am no more than five or six acres from a house or road in any direction yet feel, for one moment, panic, a vestigial reflex from a time before we'd converted most wilderness into subdivided house plots, before industrialization began to separate us from the natural world, homogenizing everything into a bland comfort, pumping out greenhouse gases that may one day render winter obsolete. A puff of wood smoke blows toward me and I move in its direction, sniffing the air like a wild dog, till I'm in my backyard. Later, I share the story with my son Carl who says, "Okay, no grandkids wandering in the backyard alone."

By February, midwinter, a deep cold sets in. Kevin and I dress in so many layers to go out we feel like mummies. The wind is frequently biting, black ice everywhere, walking treacherous, but we go outside; breathe with the world, center consciousness, sila, as winter wraps that world with its frosty breath of life, and offer thanks, hope for its continuance. We hear, more frequently now, meteorologists speak about unseasonable cold here, unseasonable heat elsewhere, droughts, monsoons, mudslides. Inuit believe shaman on mystical journeys accept responsibility to atone for tribal transgressions and to restore balance in the everyday world. Outside in the dwindling light, amid skeletons of oak and maple, I mourn for our children and grandchildren, forced to take on that responsibility, atoning to the planet for the ways their forebearers have mistreated it.

By February's end, I yearn for brightness to lengthen days, become an expanding highway between shortening nights. Each winter, incremental increases of daylight after solstice are so gradual that I don't experience them, until one morning everything seems to explode into light. I envy the Inuit firmly centered in the cold, mystical qualities of a world with intermittent light. I resolve to work harder, to make these short days more productive, to further appreciate the austere, sculptural beauty of the winter landscape, to fully nourish myself with darkness, to live in the present moment.

As if to taunt me for my resolve, two days of fifty-five-degree weather appear. Ice melts from the roof, a sparkling mini waterfall. Conifers seem to suck up green from the air. Black dots, stark against the hard-packed snow, come to life; snow fleas, also called springtails. These tiny insects, beckoned from their dormancy by the late April like weather, frolic wildly echoing my own intoxication with the unnatural warmth despite knowing that this is global climate change puncturing holes in the natural order of things. I reread an Inuit poem: "Oh how entrancing, oh how joyful, I lay me on the ground sobbing." Over the next few days temperatures dropped to twenty, rose, and fell again.

I drive to Massachusetts to meet Carl and my grand-daughters the following week, on a forty-five-degree day of bright sunlight. We are spending the afternoon at Parker River Refugee on Plum Island, a natural barrier island of 4,662 acres of dunes, beaches, salt marshes, mini-forests of thickets and shrubs.

When I arrive at his house the snow is branded, as it is in all cities, with streaky car exhaust, muddy footprints, debris;

sun transforming it into speckled cornices of ice. However, on the shady boardwalks winding through the refugee, snow has retained some pristine element. Bright gold slits through the mixed canopy overhead, fires snow into mica-like flecks, mantles this natural world with an enticing sheen. My granddaughters want to hold it. They pull off their mittens, cup mounts of snow in their hands, watch it melt, wipe their dripping palms against their jackets, then repeat the process, oblivious to their chilled fingers.

The boardwalk is surrounded by phragmites, a sixteen-foot grass with feathery, waving tops. Rhizomes, their underground hollow stems, need little to career across marshes and this invasive species has taken over completely but their thousands of plumes fanning the air are magnificent. We break off a stem for each girl. They march along the boardwalk waving these furry flags which tower over them.

Later, we walk out to the banks where the Parker River mirrors the fiery globe of the setting sun. Life flourishes here, in the depth of winter. Ducks swim in iridescent groups, webbed feet paddling like battery-powered toys. A northern harrier surveys its territory, a moment later soaring into the air, silhouetted against the sky. I think, for a moment, it's after a duck, but perhaps discouraged by the density of these quacking water-clowns, it flies in the opposite direction. My granddaughters are charmed by a flock of red-necked grebes, heads bobbing underwater, tails wagging in the air.

Temperatures lower in the shift from afternoon to evening, and scrub oaks shiver in a rising wind. After the unseasonable warmth of the day, the twenty-or-so-degrees is sharply cutting.

"Cold," Sadie says. We nod agreement.

"Cold," Carl repeats. "Time to go home."

As we turn up the path to our car, Ceiligh points and says, "Look, the moon and the sun at the same time."

As we stare, a dense cloud of starlings appears; their dark sheen and white spots paled by the lowering light, their peculiar vocalizations drifting through the air. As if to impress us, they execute the most precise, perfect series of swoops, darts, turns; aerial creatures of such grace that we are mesmerized by their pirouettes against a backdrop of purpling sky.

"Dancing birds," Sadie says laughing and applauding.

My granddaughters watch the ballet overhead and then Ceiligh throws her arms open, begins to slowly twirl and a moment later to sing, her small voice blending with the quacks, flapping and overhead cries. Her spontaneous song seems a part of the river, the birds, the trees. She sings out loud her relationship with the Earth. The Inuit poet-shaman Orpingalik said, *"Songs are thoughts, sung out with the breath when people are moved by great forces and ordinary speech no longer suffices.... All my being is songs and I sing as I draw breath."*

A moment later, Sadie emulates her older sister, and begins to sing and spin also; two tiny dervishes, arms stretched wide to welcome the winter night.

Ceiligh sings, "I love snow. I love the moon."

Sadie chimes in with, "Love, snow, moon."

Ceilgh's song is a chant, rhythmic and hypnotic and in

the descending darkness, she and Sadie are part of winter's kaleidoscope. My granddaughters are dreaming, traveling on their own mystical journey, flowing into the coldness and fading light without fear or reservation. Watching them stirs old memories of once being a child who welcomed each snowfall that draped my Brooklyn ghetto in mystery. I blew breath again and again to marvel at the white mist, sat on my fire escape nearly every night, swaddled in layers of clothes and blanket, thrilled by the early darkness that revealed winter constellations swirling overhead.

I recently read a report stating spring now arrives fifteen to twenty-four days earlier, disrupting the patterns of migrant birds, growing plants, insects. I fear it swallowing more and more of the life-sustaining days of winter, of snow melting for the last time, leaving behind a different world: the sharp winter stars of Pegasus soaring over a sorrowful, scorched landscape. It seems to me that what I want is small, yet immense; that generations of children will hear the wind hum through winter trees, will compose songs of snow and moon, will witness the geometric sketching of animal and bird tracks over white frigid fields.

Just as we reach our car, great flakes of white begin to tumble around us; rain transformed to a state of grace. We pause, four tiny promontories of this vast Earth we are joined to. The sun, as it slips into the dark envelope of night, imbues the falling white with a final luminous radiance. The whisper of snow takes over the evening. We stand quietly then, breathing in, breathing out, breathing in unison with the Earth.

About the Author

Michelle Cacho-Negrete is an award-winning author who currently lives in Portland Maine with her husband Kevin Smith, a prominent scientist, editor and author. She was born in Brooklyn and many of her essays are about her childhood. Michelle's original degree was in clinical social work and she worked for many years with victims of domestic violence, helped establish a woman's shelter in New York, and co-facilitated a batterer education program for violent men on probation.

Four of Michelle essays have been among the 100 most notable of the year and one essay won Best of Net. She is in five anthologies, including a Norton College anthology. UTNE called her essay about George Bush and the environment excellent writing. She is nonfiction co-editor for *Solstice Literary Magazine*. **Stealing: Life in America** is her first book.

Publishing Credits

These Essays have originally appeared in the Following Magazines:

"Heat" *The Sun*, issue 337, 2004 - One of The Most 100 Notable of the year, 2004

"Season of My Grandfather," *The Sun*, April, 2008 - One of The 100 most Notable of the year, 2008

"Stones," *The Sun*, April 2009 - One of the 100 most Notable of Year, 2009

"Winter," *Contrary Magazine*, Autumn Issue - Thoreau's Legacy, an anthology: American writers address global warming: October, 2009

"Stealing" *Solstice Literary Magazine*, Winter 2010 - Best of The Net, 2010 - Solit Selects, Five years of Diverse Voices, 2015 -

"On the Fire Escape" *Silk Road*, Autumn, 2011 - Persimmon Tree - Pushcart Prize Nominee

"Hair" *Solstice Literary Magazine*, Spring, 2012

"First Husband" *North American Review*, summer, 2015 - One of the 100 most Notable of the year, 2015

Roses at The End Of Summer, originally published as "And Passion Most Of All," *The Sun*, 2005.

"Rejection" *SNReview*, Spring, 2013

"The Country of the Past" - *Adelaide*, Summer, 2017

"Street Kid" *Silk Road*, Winter, 2016 - Pushcart Nominee

Made in the USA
Middletown, DE
28 October 2018